Imitate Me !

Eph. 5:1
Imitate God as dearly beloved children

D. Sterling Harlow
Ephesians 5:1

What does it mean to imitate God?

To Chisk   I love your heart for
the Lord, keep up the worship.
In Christ
Duane Harbor

Dedication

I *dedicate this book to my children, Shanna, Reina, and Darrin, who live with the memories of all the times I made wrong choices that caused them pain, and also to my wife, Marlene, who has stood by me through it all and has been my constant source of encouragement. Without Marlene, this book would never have been written.*

Table of Contents

Introduction

To his disciples, Jesus said, "Follow me" while He was walking this Earth and teaching His followers what His principles and virtues were. For three years, He filled them with His words and ideas, with His wisdom and hopes for mankind. But it was not until after His death and resurrection that He said, "Imitate Me."

There is a major difference between a follower and an imitator. Crowds followed Jesus everywhere He went, seeking healing and deliverance, watching to see the miracle show that was taking place and to see what He might do next. Many were watching these things as entertainment. They were also looking to see if He could truly be the Messiah who would set them free from Roman rule and establish His kingdom on Earth.

Today, there are still crowds of His followers filling churches all over the world, but there are few who are *imitating Jesus*. Lack of relationship, lack of knowledge, and lack of understanding (or possibly fear of the unknown) stop most from carrying out the command of God to *go out* into all the Earth and imitate Him. Followers are still looking for someone to do something miraculous. They are following the views of the church they were raised in or the views of a particular person who is currently high in the Christian ratings, but they are not doing the things that Jesus did.

We, in the body of Christ, have seen over and over that the size of a church has little to do with the character of its leader. It is very inconvenient and at times uncomfortable to imitate God. Yet there was one person who got this message. Paul, in many of his writings, made statements like this: Follow me as I follow Christ; or Imitate me. At times I have had the thought, how bold of him and maybe even a little bit prideful of him. But not so, this is exactly what Jesus had in mind and Paul got it. We are to imitate God in all we see Jesus doing. This is done by learning about Him from Jesus.

What does it mean to imitate? To do the very same things that Jesus did with the same heart attitude that He had and to get the same results that He got. What did He do, and what was His heart attitude? It is my sincere desire that we discover these great truths as we look to His Word and His ways together.

Duane Harlow

God?

B ecause you have chosen to begin the process of reading this book, I assume that you, at the very least, believe that there is a God and that you have a desire to continue the process of growing and developing into all that God has created you to be. I also assume that you believe that God, the Son, and God, the Spirit, are one with God, the Father. I will be directing you to all three of these representations of the Godhead as we move forward in our study.

Let us assume, as I do, that the Holy Spirit is, in fact, the author of the Bible, both the Old and New Testaments. Let's also assume that the Spirit of God has spoken His words into the hearts of men, and that men inspired by the Holy Spirit wrote down what they heard the Spirit saying. If we believe that this is truth, then we can put Ephesians 5:1 in first person and say that God is calling us to imitate Him. "Be imitators of God therefore as dearly loved children" (Ephesians 5:1). This does not appear to be just a good idea but rather a very direct command.

I know this may be a leap for some of you to understand, especially those who are unfamiliar with my book, ***Breaking Out of Religious Christianity***, which explains who we are in Christ. Never the less, I am convinced of this, that God doesn't tell us to do something that would be impossible for us to do with His help, such as imitating Him. He never calls us to failure!

In this book I am going to try to discover, along with you, what it will look like to be people who imitate God. No one has said that this is going to be an *easy reader*. You young people will not remember what an easy reader is. But it is what I learned to read in when I was a small boy.

Please let me explain where the title of this book came from. Some time ago I taught a home group from our church that met in my home. One evening as we began, I felt impressed to read just the first few words of Ephesians 5:1: "Be imitators of God." After reading the passage, I stopped, looked around the room, and asked this question, "What do you think it means to imitate God?"

One of our pastors was present that particular night as he had come to hear me teach. He sat there in stunned silence as I waited for someone to be the first to respond. To be quite honest, I don't recall the answers that were offered that night, but from that night on, the Lord has not let that subject depart from my heart.

Let's start by looking at the God who wants to be imitated, discovering who He is, and exactly what He wants us to do in order to look and act like Him.

Recently my wife Marlene made the statement: "How do we imitate a Father we haven't gotten to know?" If you are a WOW person, that is a good place to shout it. Are we not like the prodigal son and his brother? Have we lived in the Father's house for so long, yet we really don't know Him?

Jeremiah 9:23-24 says this: "Let not the wise man boast of his wisdom or the strong man boast of his strength or the rich man boast of his riches: but let him who boasts boast about this, that he understands and knows me, that I am the Lord, who exercises kindness, justice and righteousness on earth, for in these I delight," declares the Lord.

We must take the time to learn about God, who God is, and why we have been created, and so much more, before we can boast about Him! Who is this God? The first source I use to understand God is the Bible. It says that the Bible is the Word of God; so let's discover some of what it has to say about God.

Beginning with Genesis, we are told that God made the heavens and the Earth and everything that they contain. He created all life, both animal and plant life. And then He made mankind in His likeness. Genesis 1 and 2 should be read very carefully. He made it all from nothing! He made the Earth and set the stars in their place. He arranged the dry ground and put borders on the waters. He set the sun and moon in their places, and He created the four seasons. Then He set about making a visible man to represent Himself, who is, of course, an invisible God. "In His image and likeness He created them."

Right now it would be good if you had a great imagination. It goes on to say, He made us from the dust of the earth! No one has said that we must understand all this; we must only believe it. We are made up of dirt and water. This does get better!

"He made the earth by his power; he founded the world by his wisdom and stretched out the heavens by his understanding. When he thunders, the waters in the heavens roar; he makes clouds rise from the ends of the earth. He sends lightning with the rain and brings out the wind from His storehouses. (Jeremiah 51:15-17.)

"The Lord brings death and makes alive; he brings down to the grave and raises up. The Lord sends poverty and wealth; he humbles and he exalts. He raises the poor from the dust and lifts the needy from the ash heap; he seats them with princes and has them inherit a throne of honor. For the foundations of the earth are the Lord's; upon them he has set the world. He will guard the feet of his saints, but the wicked will be silenced in darkness. It is not by strength that one prevails; those who opposed the Lord will be shattered. He will thunder against them from heaven; the Lord will judge the ends of the earth. He will give strength to his king and exalt the horn of his anointed." (1 Samuel 2: 6-10)

I would have to quote at least a quarter of the Bible to tell you what He has done and who He is, so I'm going to let the reader dig out the many wonders of who our God is and what He has done for us.

Yesterday was Father's Day, and, as I was preparing to go to our church, the Lord gave me my very own Father's Day message. He began with the question, "Why were you created?" I responded, "For fellowship with the Father." Then He said, "Not to take anything away from the cross or what My Son did on it, but I want you understand that before the manifested Christ was on Earth, it was I who longed for relationship with my creation."

I know my theology, and I know that Jesus is the Word of God, that He was in the beginning with the Father and that the Spirit of God was hovering over creation. I also know that Jesus, God, the Son, was the last sacrifice, the great sacrifice. But it was as if the Father wanted me to know that He, along with the Word and the Spirit, desired me to have the right and privilege to relate with Him. It was the *echad* of God, (that is Hebrew for the plural of one), the oneness of God, who longed for the time that I could come into His presence unrestricted, unhindered by sin, and be invited into the throne room of the Most High for a life of relationship with Him. He looked forward to this time, even longed for it, and when He was manifested as Christ our Savior, He spoke this to His disciples: "This is my blood of the covenant, which is poured out for many for the forgiveness of sins." (Matthew 26:28) And in Luke 22:15, He said this: "I have eagerly desired to eat this Passover with you before I suffer." He was giving us the way into that throne room because He, Jesus, also had the heart of the Father beating in Him.

Conclusion! My Father, who is the great conductor of all things, loves me and wants my company so much that He paid for the ticket, got it punched, and said, "All aboard." This is a great study, and there is so much that it may take the rest of your life. So have a great time. I will go further in coming chapters, because we can't talk about imitating Him without knowing Him. Of course, God is going to be the underlying theme of this book.

What are you saying, Lord, to me?

_____

_____

_____

_____

_____

_____

_____

_____

_____

_____

2

The Journey

As I reflect on my life up to this point (in years it amounts to about 68), I'm wondering if it has all been worth it. I truly know that it has, but today I'm overwhelmed with loneliness for close family and friends. You see, in reality, I have spent most of my life leaving those I love to search for the goal of the high calling of God. My children live on opposite sides of the United States and my 8 grandchildren live in many places, both there and in between.

It seemed so simple in 1972 when I went through what I call my conversion experience. I grew up in "the church," (not as the church), most of which was wrapped up in religion, which I just couldn't seem to hold onto. In 1972, things changed forever. I got what I refer to as being *really saved or born again again*. All I wanted from that point on was to serve Jesus. And, whatever that meant, I would go on to do it with all my heart. Yes, I suffered stumbles and falls, as all of us do, but for the most part I have been filled with the mission and wonder to go and become all I can be in Christ. The cost of this pursuit has been great. In my fumbling around, trying to discover what it means to be a *Christian,* I have lost most of my close family ties. I have three children, eight grandchildren, and a wonderful wife. I didn't ask my family if this is what they wanted, I just went for it.

What do I mean that I've lost my close family ties? My son is in Oregon with his wife and four children doing a great job of building his life. One of my daughters has been in Texas at Christ for the Nations working on the next step for her life, and my oldest daughter is in Florida rebuilding her life. I'm very proud of all of my children. They have had to live through being abandoned by their father (me) for a time and then abandoned by their mother, who was killed in an auto accident. Then they grew up as the children of a pastor who didn't have as much time for them as they needed and with a stepmother. My wife and I loved our children very much, but they had to share us with so many others that they didn't get as much of us as they wanted.

My wife, Marlene, and I are now living in Colorado. We are searching for the meaning of our existence and the reason we are here. We know what the original plan was for us to come to Colorado. But that meant leaving behind 59 years in California and our 30+ years of ministry there. We only came to Colorado for a 1-year commitment, and it is now going on nine years. I had been working for my brother-in-law at a job that I was very thankful to have, but he was killed in a freak accident about 4 years ago. After working for a little over a year with my niece and nephew who were trying to fill his shoes and take over the business he left, I began wondering, "What does this have to do with the call I have on my life?" I didn't have the answers but I knew who did. When He called us here, He said it was for my calling. I'm still trying to work that out.

All we've done since we've been here is to talk about California and how we miss it and how we want to get on with our lives, yet it would seem that God has another direction for us to travel. It was in 1978 that this journey really took another turn for me. It seems that God was not impressed with my ministry and wanted to exercise more input into my life and ministry.

God spoke to me while I was sitting in my church office in Ramona, California. I was in the process of writing my sermon for Sunday and was busy taking down one of hundreds of good teachings I had in my library from Butch (Reverend Robert Pluimer) and Buddy (Pastor John Suitor), the two pastors most responsible for who I was and whose teachings I had been using for the past 3 years. They trained me and raised me up to be a pastor (sort of, as the process never seems to end), and then they sent me down to San Diego to pastor my first church.

God had the nerve to tell me that He wanted to know what I believed. He spoke to me and said, "Duane, I want to know what you believe" (with the emphasis on *you*). How's that for a paradigm shift? He wanted me to have a better grasp on what I was teaching. In fact, He wanted me to teach my own stuff. Well, have you ever heard of such a thing? I hadn't! The fact is that He was going to teach me His stuff. From that time on, it has been my Bible and me. I have never taught anyone else's sermons since that day. Don't get me wrong. I've heard a lot of good teaching since then, and I'm sure that much of it has become a part of my life, but only because the Holy Spirit has put a reemphasis on it to me from God's Word. So I'm sure some of it has found its way into my teachings.

Today, my melancholy when beginning to this work, has to do with the fact that we had a worknight last night at our church. The one we attend now is called Freedom Church, which used to be called Springs Harvest Fellowship. I am not pastoring a church at this time, but am enjoying being apart of some ones else's work. What I found out was that I cannot do the physical work that I used to do, and this morning I found out the price I will have to pay when I try. Getting older is not all it's cracked up to be. It hurts! I think I am hearing the voice of God to "leave the physical work for the younger ones."

God is so good. I was just thinking, Lord, you have given me the ministry of encouragement, but right now I'm the one who needs to be encouraged. The phone just rang, and it was my wonderful wife. Hearing her voice always encourages me except, of course, when she's upset with me. Oh, you say that you don't have upsets in your marriage? Well, will you please counsel me and tell me how that is possible? It's been 37+ years now, and we are still trying to work out that oneness principle. I wouldn't have it any other way. Check and balance, or fulfillment, however you want to put it. One in Spirit, but two separate individuals. It is the mystery of the church.

Marriage is one of the growth processes God has put into our lives. You either grow to life or die to marriage. What a wonderful gift you have given me in my wife, and I truly thank you, Lord. Before you think I'm wacko, let me just remind you that growing into all we can be in Christ is a lifelong mission. I say "mission" because it is a call from God, and it is a lot of work, but we are gaining on it every day. Of course Marlene lifted me up, and I am now seeing things in a more positive way. We truly do need one another.

It has been more than 30+ years since I began to pastor my first church, and I wish I could say that I wouldn't change a thing, but we have come a long way in understanding who we were created to be. I never dreamed that life could take all the turns and twists that it has. I would have been happy to pastor that one church and love all those wonderful people for all these years, but I had a whole lot of growing up to do.

Hindsight is so accurate as I look back at every change the Lord has lead me through. I seemed to have looked at each one as a disruption on my life, but now I can see that the Lord had a purpose in each one and that He was leading me into and out of many changes. These changes could have been so much easier if I would have let go sooner. I had to hold on and prove that I knew best. Why don't we take the first hint of the gentle nudge that comes from the Holy

Spirit? It would be so much better for everyone. I guess that is why change is sometimes referred to as "smarting." Easy or hard, God will teach us what's on His heart for each one of us.

With all the growing and changes over these many years, I wonder how they can fit into a 5'8 ½" frame. I should be at least 10 feet tall by now, and there is still so much more to learn. My prayer for you is that it won't take you 68+ years to get comfortable with who you are. Come to grips quickly with the fact that you need to love the unique individual that you were created to be. God made you as He did, on purpose, so you could fulfill the special plans and destiny He has just for you. Your destiny awaits, and it is awesome!

What are you saying, Lord, to me?

_____

_____

_____

_____

_____

_____

_____

_____

_____

3

What Do We Know about God?

W hat is it that we know about God? The first thing that pops into my mind is that He is God and I am not. Oh, where do I come up with such deep truths? What this says to me is that we must try to keep "the us" out of our first look at God. This is not easy, and we may find it very difficult. Our God is all about Him in me and me in Him. Do some reading in John 17, and you'll see what I mean.

Looking at God is similar to looking at the sun. You can't do it directly. You must use something to shield your eyes. When God gave Moses the Ten Commandments and God wanted Moses to see Him, He had to hide Moses in the cleft of a rock so Moses could only see His backside as He passed by. "Then the Lord said, 'There is a place near me where you may stand on a rock. (*If you don't understand this, it is referring to Jesus) When my glory passes by, I will put you in a cleft in the rock (*in other words, I will hide you in Christ) and cover you with my hand (*again, Jesus) until I have passed by. Then I will remove my hand (*this happened on the cross) and you will see my back; but my face must not be seen.' " (Exodus 33: 21-23) *Parentheses are all mine. I couldn't resist.

Many people (including myself) have seen Jesus, but the only safe way I know of to look at God the Father is from the Bible. Now the Bible says that Jesus is the exact representation of the Father so, if you have seen Jesus, you have seen the Father.

The Bible is the inspired Word of God, the book He left for us to live by. "Inspired" means "under the influence of." Webster's New American Dictionary's number one definition defines inspired as this: "to influence, move, or guide by divine or supernatural inspiration." So, we believe that the Bible is the inspired Word of God. Of course, if God chooses to reveal Himself to you in any form, this is also very inspired and will definitely change your life.

When we look at Genesis, we get the idea that before the world was created by God, there was nothing! Nothing at all but God! "Genesis" means "the beginning," before which nothing existed.

Genesis 1:1 says, "In the beginning God created the heavens and the earth." So we get a quick glimpse into pre-creation, but there is nothing there to see. Why did God create the heavens and the Earth and all life? Even after all these years of studying the Bible, all I have been able to come up with is that He wanted to make a place for a people who would love Him for who He is, a people to whom He could pour out His love. Then He placed them in a beautiful, secure environment. Mmmmm? I think there are several life applications here, but no, we can't go there yet, remember? We must try to keep us out of this for now. What He wanted was a family. Someone who would go by His name, someone to whom He could give an inheritance.

Where would I get such an outlandish idea that I could think on the level of how God thinks? Simple, I have read Genesis 1:26. "Then God said, 'Let us make man in *our image*, in *our likeness*, and let them rule over the fish of the sea and the birds of the air, over the livestock, over all the earth, and over all the creatures that move along the ground.' " Now, if we accept this, then we can assume that when God created us to be like Him that He put at least some of what was in His mind in our minds. Also there is

I Corinthians 2:16, which says, "but we have the mind of Christ." Are you following me? He made us to be in *His image and likeness*, so we can assume that He has a mind and that He gave us one like His. This means that we have the ability to think and act like His physical representative, Jesus. Or, in other words, we are now the physical representatives for God. Hebrews 1:3 says, "The Son is the radiance of God's glory and the exact representation of his being, sustaining all things by his powerful word." And, it is this Jesus who is our model for Christian living. I don't believe this means we are divine, but that He is divine and His Spirit lives in us. So we have the divine in us, and He is trying to get out through us. Oh, oh. I am finding it very hard to keep the *us* out of this.

God has made it clear that He has always wanted to be with His created beings. Evidently, He walked in the Garden of Eden with Adam and Eve. Genesis 3:8 says, "Then the man and his wife heard the sound of the Lord God as he was walking in the garden in the cool of the day, and they hid from the Lord God among the trees of the garden." Trying to hide continues to be a common practice to this day. Right? Darn, there I go again. I guess I'm not going to be able to keep *us* separate from our discussion of God. Truthfully, I never intended to, because it's all about Him and who He is and who He made us to be.

Did you notice that in Genesis 5:3 it says, "When Adam had lived 130 years, he had a son in his own likeness, in his own image; and he named him Seth." God passed on perfection to Adam, and Adam passed on his sinful likeness to the rest of us. We should stop right here and thank Jesus that we don't have to live in that sinful state. We'll talk about that later.

Over and over again we see God interacting with man and in some very unusual ways. I think we must look at Matthew 1:23, which says: "The virgin will be with child and will give birth to a son, and they will call him Immanuel," which means, "God with us." In verse 21, Joseph and Mary gave him his name "Jesus," and in verse 23, they said who he truly is. God with us! God with us! I have to say this over and over so my mind can grasp it. The God of eternity, the one true God, revealed Himself to us, or came to us in the life of a child. He wanted to experience life as we know it here in this world of time and space that He created for us and then to model for us how to live within it. The Life, as the Word of God calls Him, came into our world to show us the way. This is true love-that He would come to us to show us the way to once again be rightly related to the Father. This exemplifies the Father's love for us and His great desire to have a relationship with His creation.

Looking at Exodus, we can see that God Himself gives a brief explanation of who He is. "And he passed in front of Moses, proclaiming, 'The Lord, the Lord, the *compassionate* and *gracious* God, *slow to anger, abounding in love and faithfulness, maintaining love to thousands*, and forgiving *wickedness, rebellion* and *sin*. Yet he does not leave the guilty unpunished; he punishes the children and their children for the sin of the fathers to the third and fourth generation.' " (Exodus 34:6-7) He says that He is compassionate, gracious, slow to anger, He abounds in Love, He abounds in faithfulness, He loves thousands, He forgives wickedness, He forgives rebellion, and He forgives sin.

I think the New Testament captures the heart of this view of God in Galatians 5:22: "But the fruit of the Spirit is love, joy, peace, patience, kindness, goodness, faithfulness, gentleness and self-control. Against such things there is no law." Where it refers to the Spirit here, it is, of course, speaking of God, the Spirit. So, then, we get to see both the Old Testament view of God and the New Testament view. It appears that it doesn't change from one to the other. "God is the same, yesterday, today, and forever." Oh, forgive me. I misquoted that, didn't I? "Jesus Christ is the same yesterday and today and forever."(Hebrews13:8). But, again, this is referring to God, the Son, who we know as Jesus, the Christ, so is one different than the other? Only in our minds. For in reality, God is God no matter which form He chooses to use to express His love and to interact with us.

What are you saying, Lord, to me?

_____

_____

_____

_____

_____

_____

_____

_____

_____

_____

_____

_____

The Journey Continues

W hack, and the fight was on! Another step into my manhood had just begun. This is what I called a real John Wayne battle. Fists and arms flying, chairs overturned, and the kitchen table pushed across the floor into the wall. In the background, I heard a woman screaming (my mother). This event could have been a part of many John Wayne movies I watched as a child. Chairs flying, people screaming, but, alas, it was not. I could feel this one.

Sibling revelry had popped up once again. My brother, Ron, and I were mixing it up in the kitchen of our house. Many times in the past, we had had problems, but this time was different. I had never really fought back before, so that was a first for me. I was fighting back!

I was 15 and my brother was 19 and he had always just been able to hit me whenever he chose with the result that I would run or submit. But that day something changed, and, even though the outcome of the fight was much the same, the outcome of that whole event was much different. We would never fight again. Funny what goes through your mind at times like this. He had me in a head-lock, punching me in the face, and all the time I was thinking that he loved me. You see, I know that he's pulling those punches and really doesn't want to hurt me much. We were actually bonding, and from that point forward, we became co-combatants in the war of life. Evander Hollyfield I'm not, but, when it was over, there was a new respect on Ron's face for me.

There have been many events in my life which, when they were over, would never leave me the same again. In 1947, I first accepted Christ into my life, and I believe that altered history for all time. It certainly did mine.

All of us are on a journey. In the natural, the journey begins at birth and ends at death. In reality, it's a race against time. We never know how much time we are going to get. That's why we must understand that the journey is vital to who we will become. Good or bad, we are influenced by everything that happens in our lives. From the first school, first kiss, first car, first fight, first mar-riage (many fights), first child, first divorce, and so on. Thousands of events happen and are happening in each of us, and they are all meaningful. We are being shaped and molded into an adult with a particular mindset. Mindsets, perspectives, or paradigms are change-able, but it takes a new view, a new revelation, and some real work to do it. This is what we come into the kingdom of God with and what the Holy Spirit has, with our help, the opportunity to adjust.

Military service and Vietnam and its aftermath did much to shape me. Those who we meet affect us greatly. Had I not met Mike while I was in the Navy, I most likely would not be married to Marlene now, though they never knew each other at that time. Mike became a hair stylist when he got out of the military service, and he influenced me, so when I got out of the Navy, I also became a hair stylist. Because of this, many years later I would meet Marlene as one of my clients. I say this to illustrate how important events in our lives can be. After 37+ years of marriage to her, I can't and don't want to imagine life without her.

The year 1972 was a year of great change. Our marriage was less than a year old and it was not going well. We were already looking for a way out. Instead, God had a different change in mind. With a commitment to Christ for Marlene and a fresh commitment to Christ for me, God started a whole new season in our lives. Instead of a divorce, someone gave us Jesus. What an awesome gift! This was and has been a major event and a paradigm shift that have altered the course of both of our lives and the lives of many others.

Who we are and what we have become are tied to everything we have experienced. When Jesus chose the 12 disciples to follow Him, He didn't erase their past and start over. What we didn't see Him do is take the 12 and hollow them out and stick his Spirit into each one and then say, "Now you're ready for My service." No, what He did was to take each one and say, "All that you are, all that you have been through, all of your faults, pains, failures, and victories, all of your past and all of your future, I will use for My glory. Nothing in you and nothing about you do I want to hinder our relationship. I will use it all.

"Much of what you have been through has polluted your life and has caused you great pain. What changes I (God) make in you will seem like they came from a good choice of yours. I work from the inside out. I will need one thing from you. I need you to give me your free will. I will not violate that nor will I fight it. You must freely give yourself to me."

He takes us right where we are and begins to go forward. Although we are brand new creatures in Christ, we must still contend with our souls and bodies. Rightly aligned we are Spirit, Soul, and Body. The faithfulness of God is so great; He takes all we are and begins the process of conforming us or recon-forming us into His image and likeness. I say recon-forming because He had already made us in His image and we worked hard to undo it. He uses the good, the bad, and the ugly, and somehow it can all bring glory to Him. He grooms, heals, and restores us, and He does this all in His timing and in His supernatural ways.

It took many events in my life for me to become a man, and many more for me to grow into what was my boyhood dream of being a pastor. The first pastor I had (I can no longer remember his name) was my first real hero. I can remember saying to someone,

"When I grow up, I want to be a pastor." Many years of rebellion and running in the opposite direction would take place before that would even become the remotest possibility, but it was inside of me trying to get out. A seed had been planted by God, who then spent years watching and waiting for this young man to grow to a place of complete helplessness. Once there, I saw what a mess my way of doing things had made for me. There was nowhere else to go, and "I found Him." What a joke! You know this is what we do today. We run around looking, searching for something, maybe it's even Jesus, only to finally discover that He was never hiding. He was there all the while, calling, wooing, waiting for us to be still long enough so that we might hear His voice.

When I became a pastor, I discovered that, although all the teachings that I had been blessed with by some very good Bible teachers, (learning all the wonders of the Word of God) was great, God wanted me to continue my journey and to discover for myself what His Word had in store for me. This was a major paradigm shift for me. I had trusted and relied upon those teachings of others. To think that I now had to do this for myself was scary. After all, I was now a pastor and responsible for sharing His Word with many others. Would I get it right? Would I teach heresy? Although I have made many mistakes over these 30+ years of pastoring, God has very graciously pardoned my blunders as I hope those I have had the privilege to teach have also done.

During the past 10 years, the journey seems to have taken on a much faster pace. No longer does God give me weeks to change once He has shown me some area of my life that He thinks needs to be adjusted. It's as if He were saying, "This is what I want you to do; now do it!" I know that it comes with more grace than this, but it seems like He is demanding more from me sooner than He had done previously. Today, what I am writing about, I am living through.

My walk with the Lord began while my mother was still carrying me in her arms. I remember a church in San Fernando Valley, California, which I believe was called, "The Little Church of Sherman Oaks." They had a very lively pastor. Our trip across the valley to church was always special. Our car was a very used 1932 Plymouth. That trip took forever, but mom loved it, so off we would go each Sunday morning.

The pastor played the guitar and the harmonica at the same time and when he was done, he would preach. I recall standing next to a drinking fountain in one of the halls; it was one of those old white porcelain type of fountains. That was where I recited my first memory verse, John 3:16. This was during World War II or just after. I remember one of my friends at the church had just lost his father in the war. It was a difficult time for my family and friends.

From there we went to a Brethren church which was closer to our home. We could walk to that one. We didn't have to use faith that Old Betsy, as my mom called her, would get us there. There I was baptized and this is where I heard the call of God to be a pastor.

We, then, moved on to the First Baptist Church of Van Nuys. This is now part of Church on the Way. Then, when I was 14, my mother got married again. She had been raising all four of us by herself. I don't know how she did it. It must have been God. We then moved to Covina, California, and attended the First Baptist Church of Covina. Marriage agreed with her and they were married 48 years.

At this time in my life, church collided with my teenage years, and there was another great change that I (like so many others) went through. Girls, drag racing, (to this day I am not sure which one was most important) hot rods, (remember it was the 1950's) dancing, parties and hormones all got in the way of my walk with God, and for many years they held sway over my life. It wasn't until after the military, Vietnam, and the mess of doing it my way, that I *found* (which one was really lost) the Lord and began to try things His way.

Another life-changing event just happened last year. I finally received the blessing of a Father over my life. Growing up without a father didn't afford me the opportunity to receive a father's blessing, and, when my Mother remarried, it still never happened. I presided over the funeral for my stepfather when he was almost 101 years old. In the 48 years he and my mother were married, he never became a real father to me. He was a good man and loved my mother, but he had already raised his children. And, of course, I really wasn't into the relationship with a father figure after 14 years of being without one. The funeral was on a Saturday, and the following day at church, my pastor (Dutch Sheets) did something so special for me and for the whole church that I believe it changed many lives. He called the entire church forward, one row at a time and said that he and his wife, Ceci, were going to release a father's and a mother's blessing on each one who came forward.

When he did this, he made the statement that they would not be able to pray long over each person because there were so many, but that they would only release a blessing as they came by. When pastor Dutch was about four people away from me, I began to be filled with sadness and pain coming up from somewhere very deep within me, and I began to sob. The closer he came, the more I sobbed till the pain I was feeling became a cry from my heart. Then, just before he got to me, his wife Ceci bent over and whispered something in his ear. I was told later that she reminded him that I had just buried my stepfather the day before.

When he came to me, he pulled my head into his chest and just held me and prayed a father's blessing over me, while, I, ruined his suit. This had never happened to me before. After 65 years, a Father figure, one that I truly respect, blessed me and said he was proud of me. I do not remember ever being held by any father figure and feeling so loved. It has changed me. An authority figure that I truly respected released me from an orphan spirit and blessed me with a powerful blessing. I believe this has given me the opportunity to step up to a higher place in my journey of becoming all I was created for. I could now understand sonship from a new and real perspective for the first time in my life. And this process goes on.

What are you saying, Lord, to me?

_____

_____

_____

_____

_____

_____

_____

_____

_____

_____

_____

_____

_____

_____

_____

_____

_____

_____

_____

_____

Two Keys to Understanding God's Word

One night recently the Lord woke me up and began a download to me by saying, " I have two keys in helping you understand the Bible from *My perspective*. It was as if He were saying, " If you want to understand My Word the way I do and the way I intended it to be understood, then you must change your view and see things from My perspective."

He began by saying, "The first key is the story of the prodigal son. You have read this for many years, but now I want you to see it from where I sit. It's important that you get My understanding on this story. The second key I will release to you is the understanding of the ministry of reconciliation. When you have my viewpoint on these two portions of My Word, then you will be able to see and understand my perspective on the rest of Scripture."

Keys, by their nature, are designed to unlock things that have for some reason been locked up. I know this is a simple truth, but God wants to set some of us free to see the view from where He sits. This can change your life if you will let it, so see with me and be free. Unless the Holy Spirit enlightens our understanding on His word with one of His wonderful keys, we will remain locked up tight and miss what He wants us to know. All we will have is the letter of His Word, missing out on His heart for us.

Key 1

The Story of the Prodigal Son: Luke 15:11

The story of the prodigal son is not just the story of one lost sheep going astray, although it is that. It is so much more than that. For many years I have read this story and have always been impressed with this father and his love for his son. A son who did not respect his home, his father, or even his own life. But today I see a larger picture. The main emphasis of the story has always been on the son, on his rebellion and sin against his father and on his humble return.

This is truly the story of the body of Christ and of our Heavenly Father's love and grace for us, His creation. Today, as I read this story, I see it as all about the Father of the prodigal son. [12]"What do you think? If a man owns a hundred sheep, and one of them wanders away, will he not leave the ninety-nine on the hills and go to look for the one that wandered off?" Matthew 18:12.

Many of us can relate to the son who believes he has finally come of age. He is in the process of searching for his own identity, and he is straining for his freedom. He can't wait for the timing of his father or that of the Lord, to bring this to pass. So he runs off with everything he owns and his portion of the family inheritance leaving behind a brokenhearted father and a bewildered, angry brother.

The brother who stayed home has many of the same problems but he is not searching for his identity like his impatient brother. Instead, he is living in resentment while his brother searches the world for who he is. Neither one has learned the truth that real freedom comes when you live in your father's house and recognize that everything in the father's house belongs to you.

We, as the church, need to hear this. If we are living in the kingdom of God, then we have access to everything the Father has provided. It all belongs to us! Don't be like either one of the brothers who felt they had to live in resentment because they didn't know what they had, or to run after it in some frantic search, only to discover you were right in the center of God's will all the time.

Another example of this is what took place in the garden with Eve. Satan convinced Eve that she had to get something that she actually had. These two brothers could have everything in the house because it was their inheritance, and it was to be used and enjoyed. We are much like this. We get saved, and Jesus brings us into a relationship with the Father. But, then, we spend the rest of our lives trying to earn everything else or to search for something that we perceive we still need.

I was much like the first brother. I ran from my father's house when I was 17 years old and spent everything I had on the things of this world. One day this Jonah was, figuratively, puked up on a beach, and I realized what a mess I was in and what a mess I had made of my life. And not just my life but of the lives of others who were close to me. I discovered that I had no idea what real happiness was or where to find it. Humbled and wasted, I came back only to find the Father had been watching for me and couldn't wait to embrace me and welcome me back into His kingdom of life.

How do we imitate a Father we have never really come to know? Many of us are not unlike the prodigal son or his brother. We've been living in the Father's house, but we have never really known Him. So I ask you, "How can we imitate Him?"

This story is about the absolute love of the father for his son. From the time the son left until his return, his father never quit looking for him. He watched and waited, ready at the least sign of dust on the horizon to run and greet him and bring him home. Please understand with me that God our Father, to demonstrate His great love and desire to be in relationship with us, is using this story for you and me, the body of Christ. It's all about His willingness to welcome us back each time we stray from home no matter how long it takes.

Approval is something we all want and need. We're hungry for it, not realizing that we already have it from the One who hand-crafted and designed us. Colossians 1:12 says this in part: "Who has qualified you to share in the inheritance of the saints in the kingdom of light." This is the Father saying to us that we have been *qualified by Him* to live in His kingdom. Then verse 13 says, "For He has rescued us from the dominion of darkness and brought us into the kingdom of the Son He loves, in whom we have redemption, the forgiveness of sin."

Wow! He rescued us, and we didn't even know we needed it. This is not only good sermon stuff, but also, this truth, if we can see it, will bring to us true freedom. Is there anyone else any higher to qualify us to live in the kingdom of God? For those of you who may be unsure how to answer, I'll do it for you. No! "Then the King will say to those on His right, 'Come, you who are blessed by My Father; take your inheritance, the kingdom prepared for you since the creation of the world.' " (Matthew 24:34) Since the creation of the world! As we read this, how many of us have ever truly seen that? This is a part of what we were made for. The Father has given us the Kingdom, and we are still in line begging for bread.

Here is an illustration from real life. A few years ago my wife and I got a blessing. We got an all-inclusive week in Mexico. We are not world travelers so we didn't understand what all-inclusive really meant. Most of our trip was almost gone when we discovered that the bar was included. Marlene and I are not drinkers but we had seen many people with what looked like special coffee drinks but, because we really had very little money, we tried to look the other way. Well, this bar had all kinds of flavored coffees and they were free. Well, sort of. They were included. In relation to my story, many of us have lived in the Kingdom of God for years and have not understood what is included. We miss so many blessings!

It's important that you get this. What the Father does is extend a personal invitation to us to come back and live with Him in the garden. I see the garden as a type for the kingdom of God. The kingdom of God is not a place but it is *God's rule* on Earth. "Come back and live under My rule on Earth, under My blessings, under My glory, and in My love and acceptance. Everything I have is yours. Eat from the fruit of the trees: Love, Joy, Peace, Patience, Kindness, Goodness, Faithfulness, Gentleness, Self-control, Healing for the Nations, and Personal Healing. Drink from My River, and never thirst again. I am the water of life!"

The Father is waiting to see you turn around and begin to walk home. When He sees you turn (which is a sign of repentance), He will run to you and embrace you. He will put His colors (robe of righteousness) or (you who were once gang members can relate to this) on you and put again His sign (signet ring) on your finger. He will call for new sandals for your feet, which speak of a new foundation, or in this case, a restored foundation. "If you turn your foot because of the Sabbath, *from* doing what you please on My holy days, and call the Sabbath a delight, the holy of Jehovah, honorable;

47

and shall honor Him, not doing your own ways, nor finding your own pleasure, nor speaking *your own* words, then you shall delight yourself in Jehovah; and I will cause you to ride on the high places of the earth, and feed yourself with the inheritance of Jacob your father. For the mouth of Jehovah has spoken." (Isaiah 58:13-14. NKJV) *Please see note. Don't be afraid. This is not legalism; it's the heart of the Father for us. He wants us to live in His blessings.

All this means is that you are accepted back into the family and you now have a new *full share* of what is in His kingdom. Your past is exactly that. Past! Know for sure that we are fully forgiven. And when the Bible says that we are now joint heirs with Christ, that is the truth. (Romans 8:17). I will return to this key in later chapters.

Key 2

The Ministry of Reconciliation: II Corinthians 5: 11-21

Remembering that our goal is to see these two portions of Scriptures from a new perspective (God's) in which we will be much better able to understand the rest of the Bible, let's move forward.

Here in II Corinthians 5:14 the story sets the stage first of forgiveness with the statement: "One died for all." And, because of this, we should live our lives for the One who died for us, and we are no longer to live for ourselves. Then the Bible goes on to say in verse 17, "We are new creations in Christ; the old is gone and the new has come." This sounds like something we just read, doesn't it?

In Christ we are brand new. This means that we are something that has never been in existence before.

This is our redemption. He has reconciled us to Himself and then says to us: "Now you go out and do this for others in my name, representing Me! I send you as my ambassadors to tell the world that I long to have relationship with *every one* of my creations. It doesn't matter what you've spent your life on in the kingdom of darkness, I want you back, and I am waiting at the head of the street looking for you so I can bless you with all that is within My kingdom of light." Remember, we have been in hiding and out of relationship since Adam and Eve blew it in the garden. It's time for us, (the body of Christ) to come out of that place we have been hiding in for the last 2000 plus years!

This is the message He puts into our hearts when we are born again, yet so many miss it because they cannot put off the old and put on the new or because they are living in guilt and the condemnation of their lifestyles and cannot accept the complete forgiveness He is handing out. Come on, reach out and take it. It's free. I know it sounds too good to be true, but it is. Free to us, but it cost Him everything.

Hear me. Freedom is costly, but yours has already been paid for. "Praise be to the Father of our Lord Jesus Christ who has blessed us in the heavenly realms *with every spiritual blessing in Christ*," (Ephesians 1:3). Don't think that because it says spiritual blessings that it is not for you or for today. Spiritual blessings are simply God blessings, blessings from your heavenly Father.

When the prodigal son came home, the father immediately called for the robe which displayed the family colors to be put on the son and the family crest (ring) to be placed on his finger. All that he lost or spent was replaced as if it were never truly lost. Reconciliation was immediate. There were no hoops to jump through or penalties to pay, no I told you so's. Reconciliation is a complete package waiting to be accepted. As I have already said, the past is exactly that, past. And now what lies before us is a new kingdom for us to explore. We have left the kingdom of darkness and moved into the kingdom of light. What delights await us?

The brother who stayed home never knew that these things were there for the taking. Don't waste your kingdom living not understanding what has been given to you or by getting religious and trying to earn it. It's your free gift to live in. All the spiritual blessings in the heavenly places are yours according to Ephesians Chapter One. What are you waiting for?

Every work of God is redemptive. All He wants is relationship with you. Jesus wept over Jerusalem because the people didn't recognize who was in their midst. Redemption was walking the streets where they lived, and they didn't want it because it came in a package they weren't expecting. Don't you miss it! It's free and it's for you.

The love that waits for you goes far beyond anything you've ever experienced in this life. The Father's love is such that He sees only His creation and not what that creation has been involved in. The blood of Christ covers everything else. What a deal!

If you can receive this: the entire New Testament is nothing but a great big setup. That's right, I said a setup. You and I have been given the right to be reestablished in a complete relationship with God, unencumbered by sin and He has made it all possible. All that is necessary on our part is obedience to Him and to His word. Obedience is not a dirty word. It is simply doing those things that please God. You know, loving one another, being kind. The stuff He wants to do for you.

Now it comes down to us. Are we going to go out and represent this awesome God who longs for each one of His creations? Remember that not even a sparrow falls from the sky without God seeing it, nor a hair from our heads. It's with this kind of love that Jesus flowed in when He washed the feet of His disciples just before going to the cross, that He wants us to represent Him with. If we know this love, how can we do anything else?

What are you saying, Lord, to me?

_____

_____

_____

_____

The Great Exchange

O f course there were two great exchanges. The first one cost Jesus, the Word of God, His place in Heaven when He said, "I will go and be the lamb for the final sacrifice to set our creation free once and for all. I will go and live on Earth as one of them. I will live among them and be the sacrificial lamb and die for their freedom."

Now understand, this is God speaking. God, who created the Earth and everything in it, who created man and woman, was to come as a baby and die for us as a sacrificial lamb in our place. He exchanged His glory as the Word of God, (second person of the Godhead) to become one of us so that we could see and understand how God designed us to live. The *great exchange* or the divine transfer is vital to our understanding if we want to understand our God and understand how we are to relate to those around us.

One of the most important verses in the Bible is found in 2 Corinthians. It's only 23 words. That's all! Twenty-three (23) words from the Bible that change *everything*. For verse 21 of 2 Corinthians 5 says this: "He made Him who knew no sin to be sin on our behalf, that we might become the righteousness of God in Him."

Okay, what exactly does this mean? Galatians 3 gives us some light on this. Verse 13 of Chapter 3: "Christ redeemed us from the curse of the law, having become a curse for us—for it is written, "Cursed is every one who hangs on a tree."

Jesus, God the Son, died our death for us so that we could live our lives for Him. On the cross He cried out, "My God, My God, why hast Thou forsaken Me?" As Jesus became the sacrificial offering for all mankind, God the Father, had to turn His back on Jesus until the sacrifice was finished. Jesus had to die to pay the price for our ransom so that we could go free. That death changed everything for us. We, who were separated from Him by sin, could now be reunited with our Creator. No longer locked out of the garden, so to speak, we now had the right and privilege to enter into relationship with the One who made us and to live in His kingdom on earth.

We were created perfectly and without flaw, designed by God to live forever with Him. But here is the catch. Before the world was formed, God the Son was set to be our Savior. The fall of mankind in the garden did not catch the Father by surprise. Provision had already been made for His creation to be restored to Him. Listen to what this verse in 2 Timothy 1:9 has to say: "This grace was given us in Christ Jesus, before the beginning of time." God's plan for us began before we were created, even before He created time.

I am becoming more aware of the process we call sanctification. I am leaning toward viewing this as our ongoing re-creation to becoming all He had in mind for us to be. Without the process of change, without the difficulties we face in being transformed *back* into the image and likeness of God (back as we were originally created to be), without this time of trial, temptation, and failure; we could not become the strong and powerful witnesses or representatives of our God that He calls for us to be. Where would we be without grace? This grace would not be a part of our lives if we didn't need it. Mercy could not have become the cry of our heart if we had not come to know sin and the ravages it has had on mankind. To think that I could be even better than new is astounding me.

The mysteries of the mind of God boggle my understanding. "But we have the mind of Christ." (1 Corinthians 2:16) Oh my, where will that statement lead us? My prayer is, "God, continue the process of perfecting your work, for the more I know, the more I want to know. The more understanding you have given me the more of it I long for."

Here's an illustration from my life. While I was in the Navy, I was stationed on an aircraft carrier for 2 years. When we were in Southeast Asia, my aircraft carrier was what we called the flagship, or the seat of authority, because the Admiral was on board our ship, and he was in command of all the ships in that theater of the war.

When it came time for us to be cycled out and return to the United States, we had a change of command ceremony in which the flag (the Admiral's flag or sometimes called the colors) were transferred to another ship, and the seat of authority was changed to the ship that was replacing us.

This is what has happened to us. The Lord had a ceremony of sorts, and He transferred His colors from the temple, which was built with hands, to *ones* created by His hands. This shift was a transfer of the seat of authority from one temple where He dwelt to another where He now dwells. We have now become the seat of His authority on Earth for the kingdom of God! You see, true authority is not physical but spiritual. "All authority in heaven and earth has been given to me" (Matthew 28:18). And now it (He) is in us. God has chosen us to be His flagship.

My pastor, Dutch Sheets, recently said it like this. "God has established a colony for heaven on Earth. We are the outposts on earth that is to represent heaven." Matthew 6:9-10 says, "On earth as it is in heaven." This is His will, and He has given us the authority on Earth to manage this planet and our lives so that we can rightly represent our Creator. Image, likeness, dominion, rule, authority. It's all there. Read Genesis 1:26-28. Meditate on it until it gets out of your head and into your spirit. It's life changing!

Many Christians cannot understand the difference between Christianity and religion because true Christianity is all about relationship. It cannot be found between the ears; it's not a head-trip.

They relate with the written Word as information but not as with the living Word. The Word must become alive to you and not just ink marks on paper. It's not about intellectualism; it's about relationship. We are the living, breathing representation of Christ on this planet. We are now the living ink, the living paper, and the living message of the Good News (gospel) for this world we live in, because He has written it on the tablet of our hearts. This in legal terms is a contract or covenant between God and us.

"My heart is overflowing *with* a good matter; I speak of my works to the King; *my tongue is the pen of a ready writer*. You are the fairest of the sons of men; grace is poured into your lips; therefore God has blessed you forever" (Psalm 45: 1-2).

What are you saying, Lord, to me?

_____

_____

_____

_____

_____

_____

_____

_____

Does God's Heart Change?

A s I was reading Psalm 15, I had to ask myself this question, "Did the heart of God change toward us after the cross?" Many people think it did, and they are ready to deny current validity of the Old Testament and to quote scriptures on grace and mercy to you. But did it really change?

"Lord, who may dwell in your sanctuary? Who may live on your holy hill? He whose walk is blameless and who does what is righteous, who speaks the truth from his heart and has no slander on his tongue, who does his neighbor no wrong and casts no slur on his fellowman, who despises a vile man but honors those who fear the Lord, who keeps his oath even when it hurts, who lends his money without usury and does not accept a bribe against the innocent. He who does these things will never be shaken." (Psalm 15)

59

This, along with many other scriptures, represents the heart of God toward His creation. Now then it is up to us to understand what it says and how we can compare our lives to it.

First, are we talking about the life to come or heaven or are we speaking of the temple on the hill in Jerusalem? Who may live in the holy of holies with you? His answer to us on this side of the cross is "those who are blameless." This is what some people have so much trouble with today, and it's only because they don't understand who they truly are in Christ or the full work of the cross. Much of the answer comes from relationship with Jesus, but it starts with our position with God which was drastically altered by the cross.

We are blameless! What do I mean? How can we be blameless when we have lived such sinful lives? As I said in the previous chapter, He took *all* of our sin, once and for all on Himself at the cross. This is what John the Baptist said about Jesus: " Look, the Lamb of God, who takes away the sin of the world!" (John 1:29) "For God did not send his Son into the world to condemn the world, but to save the world through him." John 3:17 "God made him who had no sin to be sin for us, so that in him we might become the righteousness of God." (2 Corinthians 5:21) "It is because of Him (*God, my note from previous verse) that you are *in* Christ Jesus, who has become for us wisdom from God—that is, our righteousness, holiness, and redemption." (I Corinthians 1:30) Read these once and for all verses Romans 6:10-11, "¹⁰The death he died, he died to sin once for all; but the life he lives, he lives to God. ¹¹In the same way, count yourselves dead to sin but alive to God in Christ Jesus." Hebrews 7:27, "[27]Unlike the other high priests, he does not need to offer sacrifices day after day, first for his own sins, and then for the sins of the people. He sacrificed for their sins once for all when he offered himself." and 10:10, "[10]And by that will, we have been made holy through the sacrifice of the body of Jesus Christ once for all."

He paid the price "once and for all." Death has lost its sting because sin, which was the sting of death, has had its power over man done away with. So sin has lost its stinger, as it has been said in I Corinthians 15. No sin and no blame to those who believe! Yes, the process of the onslaught of death may still be painful, but there is no penalty in it. We can go into eternity with a smile in our hearts and confound those who are looking on.

Did you notice II Corinthians 5:21 said that we might become the righteousness of God? Well, it happened. *You* are the righteousness of God in Christ Jesus. So our position in Christ is *forgiven*, *blameless*, and *righteous*. Remember that righteousness in not something that is given and taken away. It's not something we must earn; righteousness is something that we are! (Romans 5:21 Romans 6: 18 and Ephesians 4: 24)

The remainder of this text comes to us in the process of relationship. We are being made holy, sanctified, in Christ. This process will go on in us until we are like Jesus. It's also called character building. We have been given the right to live a righteous, holy life, but the choices are ours. Will we make the right ones? Yes, we will more and more, as we keep our eyes on Jesus, the author and finisher of our faith and the one who says, "I will complete the work (*in you) that I began."

Does the heart of God change? No! His heart has always been *for* us, and His desire has always been to relate with His creation, each one of His children. You are one of His children and very special in His eyes. We can see this same truth in the Old Testament if we will look. Over and over God gives His people chances to turn from their wicked ways (those ways which are not of Him) and come back to Him. It was in Isaiah 7:14 that He announced that He (Immanuel) will be with us. First, He was with us in the garden with Him. Then, He was with us in the Tabernacle in the wilderness. Then, He was with us in the Temple in Jerusalem. And now He is with us in the Temple not built with hands. This is, of course, who we are. Each one of us is designed in His image and likeness. What I am saying is this: God has always desired to be with us. His heart has always been the same yet now we get the privilege of relationship through a price we couldn't pay, but one that He himself paid for us. God has always wanted to be with us, so He set us up so that *we* could *find* Him. What a deal! (Of course He was never lost)

Let's look for a moment at the book of Matthew. What is the message that Matthew is writing and who is it written to? As with all of the books of the Bible, we can, if we are not careful, get caught up with all the truths and good teaching material and miss the overall message.

First, Matthew set the stage by giving Jesus legal right to the lineage of David. In order for Jesus to have credibility with the Jew, He must come from the line of King David. And even though Jesus was not born of Joseph, yet because Joseph was listed as the husband of Mary, he was legally the father of Jesus in the Jewish genealogy. "[16]and Jacob the father of Joseph, the husband of Mary, of whom was born Jesus, who is called Christ." (Matthew 1:16)

Then Matthew set the stage for Jesus to be Immanuel, God with us. In order for Jesus to be able to save them from sin, He would have to be something other than an ordinary man. "[20]But after he had considered this, an angel of the Lord appeared to him in a dream and said, "Joseph son of David, do not be afraid to take Mary home as your wife, because what is conceived in her is from the Holy Spirit." (Matthew 1:20)

We also see in verse 21 that Jesus, Immanuel, is going to take away all the sin of His people. "[21]She will give birth to a son, and you are to give him the name Jesus, because he will save his people from their sins." (Matthew 1:21)

We know that the book of Matthew was written in Greek and that His audience was the Jews, who apparently were the ones on the heart of Matthew as he wrote. What a change must have taken place for this tax collector, who was hated by his own people because he cheated his people to earn more money for himself, to now be filled with compassion for them. This would be like the Internal Revenue Service of today having compassion on us and forgiving our tax debt completely. How unlikely is that?

The message here, at least in the first five chapters, appears to be the utter and complete impossibility of self-obtained righteousness through the law or by the works of man. Not only does the law make it impossible, but He even adds to the impossibility by implying that the law only covers a partial understanding and is more encompassing than originally understood.

I am going to list 6 things from the book of Matthew that prove the utter impossibility for you to attain to your own righteousness, with or without the law.

Murder: "[21]"You have heard that it was said to the people long ago, 'Do not murder, and anyone who murders will be subject to judgment.' [22]But I tell you that anyone who is angry with his brother will be subject to judgment. Again, anyone who says to his brother, 'Raca, is answerable to the Sanhedrin. But anyone who says, 'You fool!' will be in danger of the fire of hell."

Adultery: [27]"You have heard that it was said, 'Do not commit adultery. [28] But I tell you that anyone who looks at a woman lustfully has already committed adultery with her in his heart. [29] If your right eye causes you to sin, gouge it out and throw it away. It is better for you to lose one part of your body than for your whole body to be thrown into hell. [30]And if your right hand causes you to sin, cut it off and throw it away. It is better for you to lose one part of your body than for your whole body to go into hell."

Divorce: [31]"It has been said, 'Anyone who divorces his wife must give her a certificate of divorce. [32] But I tell you that anyone who divorces his wife, except for marital unfaithfulness, causes her to become an adulteress, and anyone who marries the divorced woman commits adultery."

Oaths: [33] "Again, you have heard that it was said to the people long ago, 'Do not break your oath, but keep the oaths you have made to the Lord.' [34] But I tell you, Do not swear at all: either by heaven, for it is God's throne; [35] or by the earth, for it is his footstool; or by Jerusalem, for it is the city of the Great King. [36]And do not swear by your head, for you cannot make even one hair white or black. [37] Simply let your 'Yes' be 'Yes,' and your 'No,' 'No'; anything beyond this comes from the evil one."

An Eye for an Eye: [38] "You have heard that it was said, 'Eye for eye, and tooth for tooth. [39] But I tell you, Do not resist an evil person. If someone strikes you on the right cheek, turn to him the other also. [40] And if someone wants to sue you and take your tunic, let him have your cloak as well. [41] If someone forces you to go one mile, go with him two miles. [42] Give to the one who asks you, and do not turn away from the one who wants to borrow from you."

Love for Enemies: [43]"You have heard that it was said, 'Love your neighbor and hate your enemy. [44] But I tell you: Love your enemies and pray for those who persecute you, [45] that you may be sons of your Father in heaven. He causes his sun to rise on the evil and the good, and sends rain on the righteous and the unrighteous. [46] If you love those who love you, what reward will you get? Are not even the tax collectors doing that? [47] And if you greet only your brothers, what are you doing more than others? Do not even pagans do that? [48] Be perfect, therefore, as your heavenly Father is perfect." (Matthew 5)

Matthew was setting the readers up to understand that without a savior who can remove sin completely and give them a righteousness not of their own, that they as a people, would all be lost. This reveals a grace the likes of which they had never known. "[2] For I tell you that unless your righteousness surpasses that of the Pharisees and the teachers of the law, you will certainly not enter the kingdom of heaven." (Matthew 5:20)

Not only has God the Father always wanted to be with His creation, He sent His Son who paid the price so you and I could be free from sin and become His rightful representation here on Earth! Good works and good living will not get you to heaven nor make your place secure in the kingdom of God on Earth.

What is the kingdom of God on Earth? It is simply God's rule and reign on Earth. This is what Jesus came to declare. So we, you and I, could live and preach His kingdom on earth and His kingdom to come. Over and over we see Jesus tell his disciples to go and preach the kingdom of God. He never sent them out to preach the kingdom of Jesus, but always the kingdom of Heaven or the kingdom of God.

Even though He is the centerpiece of this kingdom, He always gave the glory to the Father.

What are you saying, Lord, to me?

The True Plumb Line

In laying the foundation for the theme for this book, Imitate Me, I have chosen to use words and/or terms that are used in the building trades. What I want to communicate is that we have been given a plumb line on which to build our foundation and, for that matter, the rest of our lives. It is meant to be a simple step-by-step process. First, we lay a sure foundation, but in order for that to be correct, it must be aligned properly, and, for this, we use a plumb line.

What is a plumb line? This term is a building term used to describe a piece of line with a weight attached to the bottom so that when you hold it up, the line hangs straight down and shows vertical direction. This, then, is what you would use to align everything you want to build to plumb.

In Bible times, when people were building a building, they used a plumb line so they could cut and set the cornerstone, which was then used to line up both the vertical and the horizontal walls of the structure.

There are many uses of the term cornerstone in the Bible, and I will start there. The first use is found in Psalms 118:22, and this is considered a Messianic text, meaning that it points to Jesus Christ. "The stone which the builders rejected has become the chief cornerstone." The gospel of John confirms to us this truth. "He was in the world, and the world was made through Him (*He was the master builder), and the world did not know Him. He came to His own, and those who were His own did not receive Him." (John 1:10-11)

The next time we see the term cornerstone is in Job 38:6 where we discover that it is God who sets the cornerstone in place. As God is setting Job in his place, He mentions that it is God who sets the measurements and who stretched the line (plumb line) on it. And so we now know two things. Jesus Christ is the cornerstone and that the Father sets this cornerstone in its place.

Isaiah 28:16-17 goes on to tell us that "the Lord God is laying in Zion a stone, a tested stone, a costly cornerstone for the foundation, firmly placed. He who believes in it will not be disturbed." 17 "and I will make justice the measuring-line, (*plumb line) and righteousness the level." So now we know where the cornerstone was going to be laid, in Zion (which is the highest point in the old city of Jerusalem), and that a plumb line was used to set it correctly. Just as He said He would do, God laid Christ as the chief cornerstone, firmly planted in a tomb on Mt. Zion in Jerusalem, and it is from there that we must now build our lives from the ground up, so to speak.

In Matthew 21, Jesus condemns the chief priests and the elders of the people with one of His parables and in verse 42: "Jesus said to them, Did you never read in the scriptures, The stone which the builders rejected, This became the chief corner stone; This came about from the Lord, and it is marvelous in our eyes."

Let me take this time to introduce you to a message on the foundation. This is hot off the press as it recently came to me in a vision.

Vision:

What I saw was a statue, one like you might see in Rome. This was a big marble figure similar to the one Michelangelo did of David. That statue must have taken a person with a whole lot of God-given talent a very long time to create. It was beautiful to look at in the light. Gleaming marble and almost transparent, but I could see that something was wrong. This statue that had taken so long to create was not very steady on its foundation. Something was wrong with the pedestal it stood on. The foundation was just not right. When people would walk past it, there was movement. Barely discernable, it rocked back and forth.

What the Lord showed me was that the original foundation, which He had set in place, had been destroyed and that someone had tried to create a new one. And although it looked good to the eye, it was not as good a fit as the original foundation had been. Then He began to show me that this is what had taken place in the church. The original foundation, the one He had laid, was Hebrew and it had been stolen and destroyed. A Greek artist had created a new base for this sculpture called the church, and although it was still founded on Christ, it was and still is a Greek Christ with many new curves and twists, and not the Christ of the Jew. Christ isn't Jesus' last name. Christ means anointed one. The Emperor Constantine destroyed the true foundation of the church and built a new one. One, which was right for his own belief system. And, this changed the very core and makeup and eventually the direction of the church. The church has, thus, been on a course for Rome. But our Lord, when He comes back, will return to His own people in Jerusalem.

This is where replacement theology came into the church. Simply said, this is what much of the church believes today. God is done with the Jew, and the church has replaced Israel as God's chosen people. This is a lie placed on the body of Christ by Satan and one that the body of Christ, with its new foundation, has jumped on with acceptance.

When a Christian says that he serves a Jewish carpenter, most people don't stop to think what this means. Jesus was a Jew, and Jesus is still a Jew. Jesus is not coming back to Rome, but, when He does come back, He will come back to Jerusalem. Not only was most of the Bible written by Jewish people, but they have also been the keepers of God's word for all these thousands of years. Theirs is the true olive tree, and we are but grafted in branches. Always remember that the root supports the branches and not the other way around. Yes, they were broken off (the original branches), but if you read Romans 11, this was only for a time so that we (the non-Jew) could be grafted in and become (as Ephesians 2:14 says), "one new man." God Himself has broken down every dividing wall that has separated one man from the other.

As gentiles or nonbelievers, we have been so jealous of the Jew being called God's chosen people that we have hardened our hearts toward them, not understanding that this is what they were chosen by God for. Theirs was to keep and make available the gospel message, the word of God, for all mankind.

As I have shared previously, my wife is a Jew. She is a born-again, Spirit-filled, awesome woman of God, but for the past 28 or 29 years she has been a "Christian" believer. Oh, but how things have changed. Five years ago from this writing the Lord directed her, through one of her brothers, to go back to her roots and start again. Then Ephesians 2 jumped out at her, and Romans 11 screamed off the page.

"What are you doing, Lord?" She cried, "Being a Jew has always been filled with rejection and pain. I don't think I want to revisit that again." But, of course, Jesus just wouldn't give up being Jewish, and He was calling her back, not as an unbeliever in Christ, but now to understand Him as Messiah. We have had meetings in which Egyptians, Arabs, Jews, and Gentiles have all come together to worship the Lord Jesus Christ as one. In turn, the Arabs, Egyptians, and Jews all asked one another to forgive them for the injustices they had done to each other. It is most exhilarating and a wonderful expression of the "one new man" of Ephesians 2. My wife, Marlene, is writing her own book on what all this means, so I will stop here and ask you to look for her book in the near future.

Needless to say, our foundation is now sure, and our cornerstone, Jesus, is waiting for us with this new plumb line for us to use. And I don't hesitate to say it is Hebraic in nature. "We have been trying to understand the book of God but we don't know the God of the book." (A quote from a friend of mine)

What are you saying, Lord, to me?

_____

_____

_____

_____

_____

_____

_____

_____

How Can "We" Imitate God?

I'm not sure that this is the correct question, "How can we imitate God?" as much as it is "How *are* we imitating God?" How are we representing the One we were created to be like? I know that I have said, and I have also heard others say, that we must be models for our children. I don't think it's a big secret. We are! The key here is what type of model are we and how are we doing at being that model? This is what counts most in who our children will become.

God is and has been a model for us all along. He gave us a template in Jesus, and said to us that this is His earthly, physical example so follow after Him. So, then, what's missing? Obviously Jesus came for our salvation, but I believe that His main purpose in coming in the flesh was to teach us how to walk out this life as God would have us walk. And, also to live as He made us to live originally in the garden, so that we could rightly represent Him here on Earth.

The first thing we must understand if we hope to imitate God is: *Who are we?* We must see *ourselves* first as the most *incredible, exquisite, matchless creation* of God in the entire world. We are a created spiritual and physical manifestation of our Father who made us, and we were also created by God to represent Him on this Earth. We, along with all of creation, were given a destiny, to represent Him in every situation we find ourselves in. Whether that situation is good or bad, we are to look like Him, act like Him, and love like Him. "[14]And we have seen and testify that the Father has sent his Son to be the Savior of the world. [15]If anyone acknowledges that Jesus is the Son of God, God lives in him and he in God. [16]And so we know and rely on the love God has for us. God is love. Whoever lives in love lives in God, and God in him." (I John 4:14-16)

When the saying "What would Jesus do?" first came out, it kind of irked me. Why make a catch phrase out of what our lifestyles are supposed to be? In honesty, it also brought guilt in me for I knew that I was not living completely right. In me, it had the power in its words to convict, judge, and condemn if you were not living 24/7 for God. Then, after taking time to look at it more closely, I began to see just how right it was. What would God do in this situation or how would He handle this crisis? How would He love the unlovely? Etc.

God did not create us "just a little bit lower than Himself (Elohim) to *be* Him, but to *represent* Him, and to do that with our very own unique personality, which He created in each one of us as individuals. You may say, "How can we represent Him in our sinful lives? After all, isn't He sinless, holy, and righteous?" Good question. And the answer is yes, of course, but He didn't create us to represent Him in our sinfulness. Instead He gave us a brand new life with which we are to represent Him. We are brand new creatures in Christ, and it's as these new creatures that we are sent out by Him to be His ambassadors. It's not with the differences that we have when compared to Him that we are to present Him to the world, but it's with our likenesses. If we ever hope to imitate God as it says in Ephesians 5:1, then we have to understand that we are imitating Him in our similarities to Him and not in our differences. "⁶Whoever claims to live in him must walk as Jesus did." "¹⁷The world and its desires pass away, but the man who does the will of God lives forever." (I John 2: 6,17)

Let me go over some Scripture with you. 1 Corinthians 2 is vital to our understanding if we want to correctly represent God. The whole chapter is incredible but, for now, let's catch a broad view of what is ours in Him.

You and I are created to be like Him, and it clearly states that we can know the mind of God. In fact, it demonstrates that we can function in the power of God by learning to hear from the Spirit of God. Verse 4 says, "My message and my preaching were not with wise and persuasive words, but with a demonstration of the Spirit's power, so that (*for this purpose) your faith might not rest on men's wisdom, but on God's power." You should read the whole chapter but go now to Verses 9-12: "However, as it is written: 'No eye has seen, no ear has heard, no mind has conceived what God has prepared for those who love him—but God has revealed it to us by his Spirit. The Spirit searches all things, even the deep things of God. For who among men knows the thoughts of a man except the man's spirit within him? In the same way no one knows the thoughts of God except the Spirit of God. We have not received the spirit of the world but the Spirit who is from God, that we may understand what God has freely given us.' " This is a big Wow!

Chapter 3 goes on to tell us to quit acting like mere man. What I hear is that we are to quit acting like mere man or natural man, who does not know God, but we are to act like God because we have been given God's Spirit, and that same Spirit of God is making God known to us. When we speak about the fruit of the Spirit, it is not what is found in us, but it is what is found in the mind and heart of God that He wants us to live by. He has given us of His Spirit so that we can change our spirit to be like His. "7Get rid of the old yeast, so that you may be a new unleavened batch—as you really are. For Christ, our Passover lamb, has been sacrificed." (I Corinthians 5:7)

When I shared with Marlene about His Spirit directing us she said, "Of course." (I am a bit slow sometimes) then she said, "It's the way John (the apostle) got the book of Revelation." Then I said,

"Oh yea, (really quick; now I'm into it), and it's the way that Peter got the message on the rooftop to go to the Gentiles, and the way Paul received the Macedonian call." You get the picture. It comes by His Spirit and His will. Let His will be done on earth as it is in Heaven.

We *must* understand that we are the righteousness of God. How did we become righteous? God did this for us in Christ, at the cross. We *must* understand that we are holy. How can I say that we are holy? Because He, in His great mercy toward us, made us holy at that same cross. We *must* understand that we are the light of the world, because He gave us His light. We are the glory of the Lord because Jesus gave us His glory, the glory of God, that same glory that God the Father gave to Jesus His Son. We *must* understand that we are the temples of God and that He lives in us. And then, of course, we *must* understand that we are joint-heirs with Christ, sharing in His inheritance with Him. We *must* understand that we receive from God, the Father, by God, the Holy Spirit. I am emphasizing the word *must* here, because if we don't understand the necessity of grasping the truth of *who we are in Christ,* then we can have no hope of imitating Him with our lives or our works. And, imitating Him is what we were called for. 1 John 4:17 says it this way: "In this way, love is made complete among us so that we will have confidence on the Day of Judgment, *because in this world we are like him.*" After Jesus and the cross did their work, it is now the work of the Holy Spirit to complete the transformation of our identities.

We *must* understand that none of this is because of our own merit. No, it's all because of His great love for us and His deep desire to reestablish His original plan and purpose in us. "It is because of him that you are in Christ Jesus, who has become for us wisdom from God—that is, our righteousness, holiness and redemption" (I Corinthians 1:30)

Here is a short list of what the Lord has made me to understand as concerning who we are in Him:

We are called Son's of God.

We have the same Father as Jesus.

We have the same love from the Father as Jesus: John 17

We have been given the same Glory as Jesus: John 17

We have the same seed of God in us as Jesus, Gods DNA: I John 3:9

We are children of the light: Eph. 5:8; I Th. 5:5

We are joint heirs with Jesus.

We have the kingdom of heaven as our inheritance.

We have been sent in the same way that Jesus was.

We have the same mission as Jesus, to represent God.

We are also been given the right to forgive sin.

We have the mind of Christ: I Cor. 2-3

We, like Jesus, are not mere men: I Cor. 2-3

We were both, Jesus and I, overshadowed by the Holy Spirit and given new life.

We have been given the right and privilege to represent God and His kingdom while we are on this earth in the same way as Jesus our Christ.

We are not God nor are we Jesus, but we are His reps, His ambassadors to this world.

God's eternal work is all about us and all about Him! I know that this is a power packed statement, but it is the truth. You and I are the apple of His eye, or, if you will, the center of His focus. Think about it. The God of all creation has His mind on you. Everything He has ever done is for you, and everything He ever created is for you.

Let me paraphrase Psalm 8. "When I consider Your heavens, the work of your fingers, the moon and stars, which You set in place, it is hard to imagine that you made all this for me. You made us rulers over the works that Your hands have made, and yet when I look up at the sky, I feel so small." For me, You did this? You truly must love us with a love we still don't understand.

Oh, we understand the words. We have broken them down in the Greek and Hebrew and have been good scholars, but the substance behind those words is still trapped in a hazy fog giving us only a glimpse now and then of that awesome love. And even that small view gives us the hope to carry on in your name. We want to know more Lord, more of that love that at times seems so elusive. Psalm 145:17-20 says that You love all You have created, and we know from your Word that you created everything, that has been made.

Psalm 147:3 says, in essence, that we can heal the broken arm, but that You can heal the broken heart.

There is so much more of you that we have not yet tapped into. We want more, Lord! More understanding of all You have created us to become. Psalm 147:11 tells me that Your love is unfailing. I want to experience this kind of love in my life, and, from my understanding of Your word, I already am. The only thing Lord is that I have a hard time living in this unboundness love. We want fences, boundaries that help us feel more secure. Yet you say that in You we have been made secure. We want more, Lord! Give us more understanding. In verse 15, You said that You send Your commands to Earth, and Your Word is swift to act. Send it, Lord, not the letters, but the understanding of just what you are saying to us.

I once heard Dr. C. Peter Wagner say, "In the garden there was a time when we were holy and walked and fellowshipped with Him, and then there was a time when we weren't." It's to this former place that He has brought us back in Christ.

I hear people say that it is all about the covenant, but I now see that it goes so much farther back than that. Genesis is still the key, and the book of Ephesians leads us back there. It says so clearly in Ephesians 2:4, "Because of His great love for us." The covenant is just an expression or the legal contract for this love. When the Bible says that He will take it from the stone tablets and write it on the tablet of our hearts, it is a message to us of the intimacy He desires to have with His creation. Everything must be understood from this perspective.

Remember when I said that He had awakened me and had spoken to me that if I wanted to understand the Bible from His viewpoint, He would give me two keys for this purpose? Bear with me for a moment as I repeat just a bit, for I have more to share on this.

The first key is the story of the prodigal son. Then He said to me that if I understand this, I can understand everything else. This story is not about the son or his rebellion and repentance, but it's about the love his father has for him. If we look at this story from a Hebrew perspective we can understand what the son was saying to his father: I wish you were dead, so that I could have my full inheritance. A son couldn't get his inheritance until the father was dead, and yet that is what this son was demanding. Think with me how much this must have hurt his father. His own son was crying out for his death. And yet the father said, "Ok, I'll take the hurt, the pain of rejection, and the humility in the gates with the other fathers and let you go do what you want with your life, the life I gave you." All the plans the father had for this son would be put on hold as the father had to give way to longing and waiting for his son to get it, and, of course, he eventually did. Sound familiar? Isn't this what He has done for us?

You must read between the lines and see the heart of the father as he waits for his son's return. What was the father doing when he saw his son from a long way off? He had to have taken a position of watching for him, sitting in the gate in such a way that he could see the road. Now see what he does when that day finally arrives. He did not concern himself about what all his friends, the leaders of this small community, would think. He runs to his son-this same son who had rejected him. And the father embraces him (kisses his neck). He then calls for a robe, the ring, and sandals for his feet and calls for the fatted calf to be prepared for the celebration of his son's return home.

Did you notice what was missing in this story? Condemnation, guilt, and reproof! It's not there. Instead of what we would give him, his father gives his son grace and a full new inheritance! It's all there! Nothing missing! Now some will say that it was because of the son's repentant attitude. Not so. He never gave his son the time to ask for forgiveness for all he had done. Yes, it's about us, and, yes, the son did have a repentant heart, but the father knew this by his returning home. The reality is, it's all about the Father's incredible love and forgiveness for us!

When I came back to my heavenly Father after 16 years of living in the world, I was not very excited to come back to the same old religious environment I had run away from. I came in cutting deals with Him the whole way back. I said to God, "I don't want to give up drinking. I don't want to quit smoking; I don't want to quit going out to the clubs and dancing, etc." In other words, I was saying, "If you let me have my way, I will come back into Your kingdom." And guess what He did? He didn't reject me because my attitude was not right. He took me in. I found myself wrapped up in His arms, and I wept for a least an hour as I felt His love for this lost sheep. I finally knew I was accepted and loved. He gave me my full inheritance in spite of my attitude. Because of this love, I was able to repent. All I had to do was come home to Him. The prodigal son's belief about his father's love for him changed, and this enabled his behavior to change. You cannot change your behavior without first changing your belief system. This truth will help you in every area of your life.

As much as this seems to be about us, it's really not. It's all about Him and His love for His creation. It's all about His great passion for us. It's about Him and His grace.

Now see with me what that includes.

In Ephesians 1:18-23, Paul has got it! And now his prayer is that we might also come to understand God's plan and purpose for us. "I pray also that the eyes of your heart might be opened or enlightened, in order that you may know the hope to which he has called you, (*now get this) the riches of His glorious inheritance in the saints, and his incomparably great power for us who believe." Oh, my, what a prayer! This makes Ephesians 1:23 come to life. You and I are the fullness of Him, the body of Christ is the fullness of Him, who fills everything in every way. Christ is not complete without us. The work on the cross is incomplete without His body, and, we are not complete without understanding what that work includes.

What's the cry of our hearts? Lord, give us your power. We want signs and wonders. We want to look good when we pray for the sick, and you know, Lord, that the power to heal would make this a reality and make my ministry really explode. But what does Ephesians 3:17 say? "And I pray that you being *rooted* and *established* in love, may have power, together with all the saints." Did you see it? First, we are to be rooted and established in love. Love must be the root, and, it appears to say, the foundation for the power of God to be loosed in us. Without love, power just becomes the instrument of the enemy, a tool to foster the lust for power, and that power, without the boundary or foundation of love, is very dangerous. In other words, it is what the world uses to control its environment. Love, the love of Christ is the plumb line. Everything else must line up first to this.

Is it any wonder why the body of Christ is powerless in most cases? It's because in most cases the way we see things is that it's about us and not about God. We use the right words, but it's just a religious cry. You and I want to look as if we are the Lord's servants for healing and the gifts of the Holy Spirit, and, when it doesn't happen, and, when what we have prayed for does not take place immediately, we feel as if we are viewed as not quite up to the relationship we should have. Oh, I know none of us would admit this. Instead we would begin making excuses that healing is a process or that it's all in God's timing. Some even go so far as to say it's not God's will to heal you right now. Most of the time that is a cover-up, but God is God and all we know is that He has said in His word that it is His will to heal. However, we try very hard to come out of this looking good and feeling good about ourselves. We even think we must make God look good by making excuses for Him. Truly we must have the foundation of God's love in us if we want to imitate Him.

Why do I say that Genesis is key to understanding this? Because it is here that we find this amazing word. We were created by Him in His own image and likeness (Genesis 1:23-24). We understand from this that He put in us what is in Him. It appears that all three of the manifestations of God, the Father, the Son, and the Holy Spirit, are a part of the creation called man. Have you given this much thought?

Now, we know, that He *is love*. So, it follows that we have this love as one of the key elements in us. How could we represent Him without it? Isn't this what He calls us to do with our lives as His ambassadors? What remains for us is to allow this awesome foundation to become what we are, and, then, go out and love people in His name.

What do we mean when we say, "The presence of God is here"? What takes place when God comes into a place, a room, a situation? He brings with Him who He is: His glory, His majesty, His love, His power, His righteousness, His beauty, His grace, His healing, His mercy, His knowledge, His wisdom, His light, His authority, His life! He comes and the atmosphere changes, and the fear of the Lord comes, life changes, and the enemy flees. *Emmanuel* is here! Does He leave any part of Himself outside when He enters? Does He say that this part of Him is for now but this other part of Him is for later?

NO! God is complete, nothing missing, nothing left out. He is the supernatural, awesome creator of all.

He doesn't call us sons because He adopted us. He calls us sons because He put His life in us. We have been born again. We are brand new babes in Him, not just taped on, but He brings us to the Vine where we can be grafted in, and we, then, become one with this Vine.

Once a branch has been grafted into a tree, everything changes for that branch. Now the DNA of the tree becomes infused with the DNA of the branch. It makes something new. It's no longer just the branch, and it's not just what the tree used to be. The two have become a new "one." The fruit will not be the same as the fruit of the branch or the fruit of the tree, but will share in the strongest parts of each.

This is what God has done with us. We have been infused with the DNA of the living God (Jesus), and we are no longer who we were. We are now a new "one." We are not Jesus, even though we now have His DNA flowing through us. And the longer we stay connected, the more we will resemble Him. But now we are a new creation. We are someone who never existed before.

Our fruit will be blessed with God in us, but we will still have the individual flavor of who He made us to be from the beginning. What a deal. He forms us by hand and then puts His life in us.

God still dwells in his temple, only now it has legs. When God's temple walks into a room, He is there. All of Him has just walked in as the Ark of the Covenant, and things should, and I shout, must change! You and I are those temples, and he lives in us. We are now the Ark. We carry not just part of Him but all of Him wherever we go. So what should those who do not have Him expect to encounter when we show up? The living, breathing, walking representation of God!

Why is it that we don't see this happen when we come into a room? Because for most, we have neglected the proper upkeep of the temple. For many people, the oil for the lamp has run dry, the incense has burned up, and has not been replaced and the bread of life is stale and it also needs to be replaced. Many have allowed a veil to come again in their minds to separate them from the Holy of Holies because of guilt, shame, and sin that they are still holding on to. This veil does not really exist. It's a lie from satan. This is a great tragedy, but it is very common in the church today. The only place the veil exists today is in our misunderstanding. God will never allow that veil to separate us again.

We are the priests now, and it is our job to keep our temples clean, the oil full, the lights lit, and the bread of the presence fresh, so when we enter a room it is aglow with the glory of God. And, it is then that we can expect the supernatural to take place.

Have people become immune to the presence of God when you come by? Have you (as in Matthew 5:15) hidden your light under a bowl? Have you locked the temple doors so no one can see God, or have you simply not been told who we are? We are His priests,

His kings, His joint heirs, His righteousness and His glory. Have the fires gone out that light the way into the holy place? Call for the oil, fill the lamp, and ignite it again. The Lord has not abandoned His temple. It only needs to be tended. Let the sweet fragrance of the incense (your prayers) once again rise before Him. He waits to respond to the fervent (white hot) prayers of His saints. This takes passion, real passion for God. For example, in a recent prayer meeting at our church, while a friend of mind was praying, I had a vision:

Vision:

He had just mentioned water, and I immediately saw a picture of a stream. It was flowing into a sluice-box, one like the miners of old used. As the water rushed over the rocks and sand I could see large golden nuggets tumbling down into the box. I had the understanding that the prayers were touching the riches of the kingdom of Heaven and that we were receiving blessings of gold from God that were just a by-product of the earnest prayer that was coming up before Him.

Where does the passion come from to imitate God? This is a very good question. God is a God of many passions, so it only stands to reason that we must have passion to want to act like God, and He puts that passion in us. Then this passion comes bubbling up from somewhere deep within us. God Himself has put it there so that the passions of God will be a part of everything we do. We will have the driving force that was Jesus' as we represent Christ to this world.

Passion is the fuel of God, just like hope is the fuel for faith. Once it is ignited, it forces us out of ourselves, and we become the gospel to those we encounter. Passion comes from hope and when you connect it to faith, you cannot be stopped.

Evangelism without passion is just plain hard work, and sooner or later we run out of gas. There are so many casualities on the gospel road (burned out, empty wrecks which were once vital vessels for God) that one would wonder if it is truly worth it. It takes time, energy, and lots of love to restore just one of those fallen heroes of the faith. So starting out with the right fuel in their tanks, the right foundation, is vital. Don't get me wrong here. It takes more than passion to be prepared to share the gospel, but passion gives us the push we need when there are hills or mountains that pop up in our paths. And they will.

Do you remember the story about the two men walking on the road to Emmaus? It's found in the last chapter of Luke. These men were very discouraged. As they walked along the road, Jesus joined them. They desperately needed His presence to renew their faith and restore their hope. Even though they didn't understand at the time who He was, His presence began making a difference.

When I read stories such as the story of David and Mephibosheth in II Samuel 9, I see from that story what God has in mind for us. Or when I see Jesus' life and know that it is being played out on this Earth as a model for my life. The passion then begins to swell up to the surface and spill out on others. As I grow to understand who

I am and how much my Creator wants to spend time with me, how He wants to guide and teach me, and how He wants me to have His heart for people, passion becomes the by-product.

As you know life can at times be very difficult, and it is at these times that real passion for God helps us through it. Passion gives us the persistence to love the unlovely or, as Paul says in Ephesians, "to stand" when we don't see the results we have been praying for.

When Jesus faced the lepers, those outcasts of society, what did He do? It was His passion to see them whole again, to see them once again accepted and loved. His love for those He created, His passion drove Him to touch the unclean. He wanted to make them clean once again, and is this not the same thing we are all called to do? Imitate Him!

How can this be done? He has already made the way. He put it in us. What did He put in us? Himself! We must first ask Him to manifest His life in us, bring forth all He made us to be, all He put in us. And, then, it will be His life coming forth from us that changes the world.

I ask

The parable of the talents is all about this. Here the talents speak about our relationship with Jesus. What do we do with it? It cost us nothing but the gain is worth everything. Verse 28 of Matthew 25 says this: "Take the talent from him and give it to the one who has the ten talents, 29 For everyone who has will be given more, and he will have an abundance." The more of Jesus we can get, the better.

See with me the foundation of a New Testament teaching. Every town in the land of Israel had rabbis who would teach their disciples to become like they were. The ones who showed promise were encouraged to learn as much as possible from them, and to put into practice everything they did. Each rabbi had his own views of what the scriptures said and walked them out in their own way. This process was called the rabbis *yoke*. Does that sound familiar?

Jesus was a rabbi and in Matthew 11:28-29, He said to His followers, "Come to me, all you who are weary and burdened, and I will give you rest. Take my yoke upon you and learn from me, for I am gentle and humble in heart and you will find rest for your souls. For my yoke is easy and my burden is light." Jesus said, "Learn from me, come to me." This is different, for He was seeking out His disciples, whereas the first century rabbi was always looking for those who would seek him out. Jesus makes it easy for us. He comes to us. He takes the ones who flunked out of rabbi school and makes them His.

Paul used this same imagery with the Galatians. The religious teachers of the law had come after Paul had left that city, and they had talked the Galatians into taking their yoke, the yoke of the law, once again. In verse 1 of Chapter 5, he said; "It is for freedom that Christ has set us free. Stand firm, then, and do not let yourselves be burdened again by a yoke of slavery." They had put on the rabbis' yoke again, and Paul said that this would not lead to freedom for them, but, instead, it would lead them into slavery again. Put on the yoke of the Good Rabbi, Jesus, and you will be free. Here, Jesus represents the Son, not a slave. In order to truly understand this, you must see yourselves as sons. We are called royal priests and kings. We must get our selves out of the slave mentality and walk in what we are called to be. A slave knows his identity and he knows he is not a King or a son, nor can he act like one. We are sons of God, and we must learn this process, and then to act like it. Why do you think that Peter would dare to walk on water? He was determined to do what his Rabbi was doing.

Not only are we to learn from Him so that we can imitate Him, but we need to have ("The Stuff", as John Wimber used to call it) the anointing to get the job done. If Jesus has called us to be His ambassadors here on this Earth, it would seem very ridiculous to me to try to do this without the anointing to get the job done right. Not only does Jesus give us the anointing to do it, but He calls for us to imitate Him in doing so.

You have not only been commanded to go out and preach the gospel of the kingdom, but Jesus also calls for us to heal the sick, cast out demons, destroy disease, and to do all this while we are representing Him. We must understand that because of our redemption at the cross, our new life, and what we have been given, we - can - do – this! We have been given the right and authority to act on His behalf.

We get a peek of this in Matthew 6. Jesus gives us a model of the way He prays. And, in the last part in Verse 14 He said, "For if you forgive men when they sin against you, your heavenly Father will also forgive you." I think that most people, when they read this, just pass it up with something like this, "We are supposed to forgive people when they sin against us." But I believe we should connect this with John 20:21-22: "²¹Again Jesus said, 'Peace be with you! As the Father has sent me, I am sending you.' ²²And with that he breathed on them and said, 'Receive the Holy Spirit. ²³If you forgive anyone his sins, they are forgiven; if you do not forgive them, they are not forgiven.' " Let me rephrase this: In the same way the Father sent Me, I am sending you. We must get this! We are sent in the same way that Jesus was and to do the same things that He did.

Look with me at Matthew 10:1: "¹He called his twelve disciples to him and gave them authority to drive out evil (or unclean) spirits and to heal every disease and sickness." The events of Matthew 10 took place before the cross, and those of John 20 took place after the cross. But the message has not changed. We are all called to imitate Jesus as His ambassadors. He has put in us His temples, His life, His love, His Spirit, His Glory, and His power to be these ambassadors of His. So let's do it, understanding who He made us to be.

When we forgive people, we release them from the judgment and penalty of their sins. This is the same ministry that Jesus carried out on the cross. We have been given the privilege of participation in forgiveness.

Is this talking about when they do something against us or forgiving sin in general?

What are you saying, Lord, to me?

Having the Mind of Christ

In I Corinthians 2: 16, it tells us that we have the Mind of Christ. I have spent this morning wondering what that means. How does that work? How can I, natural man, have the mind of the supernatural Christ? This has to be a God thing. He did this. God put His Spirit in *us* and this Spirit knows what is on God's mind. Wow! Can I really know what is on the heart of God? Yes! It's a part of what has been restored to us, as we have been born again. When He created us in the beginning to be like Him, it was there. We lost it, and now when we are reborn, we have been given this awesome part of God once again.

The Bible also says that we are to put off the old and put on the new. I believe that this means that we are to put off the effects of the fall of man in the garden and put on the restoration of man that took place from the cross of Jesus forward.

Satan wants to keep us in the bondage of the fall and has tried to convince us to stay there. After all this time, it is amazing to me how many of us still listen to him. He lies, and we listen. It doesn't make sense, but he still gets away with it. Don't you think it's time we put a stop to this? Do you believe for a minute that God would put up with satan attacking Him? Aren't we God's representations on this Earth and the fullness of Christ? Why do we put up with satan's nonsense?

What was the effect of the fall of man? This is what I saw and heard this morning.

We reap what we sow!

The Fall The effects of the fall	We Stand The effects of restoration	Proof Text Scripture Verse
Darkness	Light	Eph. 5:8; 1Pet. 2:9
Lies	Truth	John. 8:32
Sickness	Health	3 John 2
Dullness	Alertness	2 Cor. 3:14
Disease	Ease	Psalm 103:3
Pain	Free of Pain	Is 53:4
Mental Sickness	Sound Mind	2 Tim. 1:7
Bondage	Freedom	2 Cor. 3:17
Locked	Unlocked	Rom. 8:15

Failure	Victory	1 John 5:4
Broken	Restored	2 Cor. 5:18-19
Depressed	Lifted High	James 4:10
Bad Thinking	Good Thinking	Phil. 4: 8
Bad	Good	Mk. 10:18/Lk. 6:45
No Authority	All Authority	Matt. 28:18/
Cursed	Blessed	Eph. 1:3
Negative	Positive	Matt. 19:26
Shame	Joy	Neh. 8:10
Guilt	Forgiven	Acts 10:43/Ish. 53:1
Condemnation	No Condemnation	Romans 8:1
Disqualified	Qualified	Col. 1:12
Sin	Righteousness	2Cor. 3:21
Stolen	Returned	2Sam. 9:
Poverty	Wealth	Deut. 8:18
Rejected	Accepted	Eph. 1:6 KJV
Weakness	Strength	Phil. 4:13
Fear	Faith	Heb. 11:1
Unbelieving	Believing	Heb. 4:3
Doubt	Trust	Prov. 3:5-6

Sometimes I find myself getting angry with those who would make Christianity so hard. The more I know about Jesus, the more I know that it is all about relationship with God though the work of Jesus on the cross. God longs for relationship with His creation, us.

He wants to invade our minds and our hearts with His love, mercy and compassion, and all the while we are being told it's about works or do's and don'ts.

Look at the list above again. Every work of evil from the enemy is only a perverted view of the blessings of God. It comes from eating from the Tree of knowledge of good and evil instead of eating the fruit of the Tree of life.

Let me break it down like this and hopefully it will help.

1. *Darkness; Light:* "[8] For you were once darkness, but now you are light in the Lord. Live as children of light." **Eph. 5:8**; and "[9] But you are a chosen people, a royal priesthood, a holy nation, a people belonging to God, that you may declare the praises of him who called you out of darkness into his wonderful light."**1Pet. 2:9**

2. *Lies; Truth:* "[32] Then you will know the truth, and the truth will set you free." **John. 8:32**

3. *Sickness; Health:* "[2] Dear friend, I pray that you may enjoy good health and that all may go well with you, even as your soul is getting along well." **3 John 2**

4. *Dullness; Alertness:* " [14] But their minds were made dull, for to this day the same veil remains when the old covenant is read. It has not been removed, because only in Christ is it taken away." **2 Cor. 3:14**

5. *Disease; Ease:* "[3] who forgives all your sins and heals all your diseases," **Psalm 103:3**

6. *Pain; Free of Pain:* "[4] Surely he took up our infirmities and carried our sorrows, yet we considered him stricken by God, smitten by him, and afflicted." **Isaiah 53:4**

7. *Mental Sickness; Sound Mind:* "[7] For God hath not given us the spirit of fear; but of power, and of love, and of a sound mind." **2 Tim. 1:7 KJV**

8. *Bondage; Freedom:* "[17] Now the Lord is the Spirit, and where the Spirit of the Lord is, there is freedom." **Cor. 3:17**

9. Locked; Unlocked:" [15] The Spirit you received does not make you slaves, so that you live in fear again; rather, the Spirit you received brought about your adoption to son-ship. And by him we cry, "*Abba,* Father." **Romans: 8:15 TNIV**

10. *Failure; Victory:* "[4] for everyone born of God overcomes the world. This is the victory that has overcome the world, even our faith."**1 John 5:4**

11. *Broken; Restored:* "[18] All this is from God, who reconciled us to himself through Christ and gave us the ministry of reconcilia-tion: [19] that God was reconciling the world to himself in Christ, not counting men's sins against them. And he has committed to us the message of reconciliation."**2 Cor. 5:18-19**

12. *Depressed; Lifted High:* "[10]Humble yourselves before the Lord, and he will lift you up." **James 4:10**

13. *Bad Thinking;   Good Thinking:* "[8] Finally, brothers, whatever is true, whatever is noble, whatever is right, whatever is pure, whatever is lovely, whatever is admirable—if anything is excellent or praiseworthy—think about such things." **Philippians 4:8**

14. *Bad; Good:* " "[18] Why do you call me good?" Jesus answered. "No one is good—except God alone." **Mk. 10:18/Lk. 6:45**

15. *No Authority; All Authority:* "[18] Then Jesus came to them and said, 'All authority in heaven and on earth has been given to me.' " **Matthew 28:18**

16. *Cursed; Blessed:* "[3] Praise be to the God and Father of our Lord Jesus Christ, who has blessed us in the heavenly realms with every spiritual blessing in Christ." **Eph. 1:3**

17. *Negative; Positive:* "[26] Jesus looked at them and said, 'With man this is impossible, but with God all things are possible.' " **Matt. 19:26**

18. *Shame; Joy:* "10 Nehemiah said, 'Go and enjoy choice food and sweet drinks, and send some to those who have nothing prepared. This day is sacred to our Lord. Do not grieve, for the joy of the LORD is your strength.' " **Neh. 8:10**

19. *Guilt; Forgiven:* "[43] All the prophets testify about him that everyone who believes in him receives forgiveness of sins through his name." **Acts 10:43/Isa. 53:10**

20. *Condemnation; No Condemnation:* "[1] Therefore, there is now no condemnation for those who are in Christ Jesus." **Romans 8:1**

21. *Disqualified; Qualified:* "[12] giving thanks to the Father, who has qualified you to share in the inheritance of the saints in the kingdom of light." **Col. 1:12**

22. *Sin; Righteousness:* "[21] God made him who had no sin to be sin for us, so that in him we might become the righteousness of God." **Cor. 5:21**

23. *Stolen; Returned:* "[1] David asked, "Is there anyone still left of the house of Saul to whom I can show kindness for Jonathan's sake?" [2] Now there was a servant of Saul's household named Ziba. They called him to appear before David, and the king said to him, "Are you Ziba?" "Your servant," he replied. [3] The king asked, "Is there no one still left of the house of Saul to whom I can show God's kindness?" Ziba answered the king, "There is still a son of Jonathan; he is crippled in both feet." [4] "Where is he?" the king asked. Ziba answered, "He is at the house of Makir son of Ammiel in Lo Debar." [5] So King David had him brought from Lo Debar, from the house of Makir son of Ammiel. [6] When Mephibosheth son of Jonathan, the son of Saul, came to David, he bowed down to pay him honor. David said, "Mephibosheth!" "Your servant," he replied. [7] "Don't be afraid," David said to him, "for I will surely show you kindness for the sake of your father Jonathan. I will restore to you all the land that belonged

to your grandfather Saul, and you will always eat at my table."
[8] Mephibosheth bowed down and said, "What is your servant, that you should notice a dead dog like me?" [9] Then the king summoned Ziba, Saul's servant, and said to him, "I have given your master's grandson everything that belonged to Saul and his family. [10] You and your sons and your servants are to farm the land for him and bring in the crops, so that your master's grandson may be provided for. And Mephibosheth, grandson of your master, will always eat at my table." (Now Ziba had fifteen sons and twenty servants.) [11] Then Ziba said to the king, "Your servant will do whatever my lord the king commands his servant to do." So Mephibosheth ate at David's table like one of the king's sons. [12] Mephibosheth had a young son named Mica, and all the members of Ziba's household were servants of Mephibosheth. [13] And Mephibosheth lived in Jerusalem, because he always ate at the king's table, and he was crippled in both feet." **2 Sam. 9** Do you see the restoration of all things for us also?

24. *Poverty; Wealth:* "[18] But remember the LORD your God, for it is he who gives you the ability to produce wealth, and so confirms his covenant, which he swore to your forefathers, as it is today." **Deut. 8:18**

25. *Rejected; Accepted:* "[6] To the praise of the glory of his grace, wherein he hath made us accepted in the beloved.." **Eph. 1:6 KJV**

26. *Weakness; Strength:* "[13] I can do everything through him who gives me strength."   **Phil. 4:13**

26. *Fear; Faith:* " 1 Now faith is being sure of what we hope for and certain of what we do not see." **Heb. 11:1**

27. *Unbelieving: Believing:* "[3] Now we who have believed enter that rest, just as God has said, So I declared on oath in my anger, 'They shall never enter my rest.' " **Heb. 4:3**

28. *Doubt; Trust:* "5Trust in the Lord with all your heart and lean not to your own understanding. 6 In all your ways acknowledge him and he will make your paths straight." **Prov. 3:5-6**

Obviously these lists are not all-inclusive nor are the scriptures I have chosen the only or best responses, but they will give you a good start if you wish to understand more.

Everywhere the enemy tries to inflict his will on us or this world, God has already provided the antidote. God has spoken to us from His word and told us that we are to live by every word that proceeds out of the mouth of God and yet we, very often, ignore His word and live in our emotions and our feelings. This is the playground of Satan. The word of God tells us to pull down the strong holds of the enemy, to put off the old and put on the new, and to think of those things that are good. So many Christians live in what I call *Experimental Christianity*. If it works out, I'll believe it. Instead of believing God because He is God, we grade Him according to what we want or believe or see. We grade Him on works in the same way we grade ourselves.

If you want a good relationship with someone, you take the time to find out what pleases that person and then you do those things. You make the other person more important than yourself. When both parties are participating in this, you discover that you also get your needs ministered too. True Christianity is about loving in the same way Christ loved. Ephesians 5: 10 tells us: "and find out what pleases the Lord." That is not a suggestion.

Since the time when Adam and Eve broke covenant with God in the garden, satan has convinced mankind that we were bound to the understanding of reaping what we sowed. He has taken this principle of God and used it in the negative and has tried to keep us in bondage to every sin that we have ever committed.

Forgiveness has become much less than its cost on the cross and, instead of Jesus paying the price for sin once and for all or as John the Baptist said, "Look the lamb of God who takes away the sin of the world," it has become selective forgiveness which depends on our emotions, our hurts and sorrows to keep it going. If forgiveness is selective then we have all been deceived and God's word cannot be trusted. In other words, we are doomed.

As one televangelist has said, "Forgiveness or grace is almost too good to be true." Well, for that matter, so is God! Without faith and the hope that the Bible is true, what's the purpose? We should all build bigger barns, drink it up while we can and be happy and die.

Remember, the Master is greater then all the lies of the angel called satan which He created. "Greater is He that is in me than he that is in the world". I John 4:4

If forgiveness isn't enough then the cross of Christ is meaningless. God dying for mankind (His creation) on the cross so that we can now be in right relationship with Him won't be enough. What more can He do?

The ultimate price has been paid and we are free from the penalty of sin, which we couldn't pay to begin with. God manifested himself in His Son as that payment. Jesus said, "If you have seen me, you have seen the Father."

In the garden we divorced God and said we want to live our own lives our way. But what did God do? He gave forgiveness so we could marry His Son. We are the bride of Christ.

Go back to the chapter on Two Keys. Key #1: When the son came home, in a sense, he became brand new. Nothing was held to his account. Forgiveness was complete. He got a whole new inheritance. His father put no guilt, no condemnation, on him.

The only unpardonable sin is not accepting the free gift of grace, which the Father gave to us before the foundation of the world in Christ Jesus. 2 Timothy 1:9

Think with me, God didn't come up with grace just to counter the works of the enemy. It's who He is. He didn't come up with the list on the right because He read the list of the left.

Satan knew the heart of God from being with Him in the heavenlies for who knows how long, and, when he fell, he became the opposite. Where God is light he became darkness. Where God is good he became evil. In the battle of good vs. evil, satan was the first fruits of evil, the father of lies, and now his entire plan is wrapped up in this statement. He came to kill, steal and destroy. There is no good in him at all! Where as satan does not have the privilege of repentance, we do. When darkness overtakes us we can call on the light and we will be changed. We are carrying the Light of the world to the world. We are torchbearers or what I call us, Glory Lamps. We have both, His glory and His light.

What are you saying, Lord, to me?

_____

_____

_____

_____

_____

_____

_____

_____

My Perspective

T his is so vitally important and because I really want you to understand this, I am going to take you on a short journey in the word of God.

The apostle Paul had the right understanding on identity. Even as he wrote his letters, we can see that his understanding of his own identity was growing deeper and deeper. This is so clear in the book of I Corinthians.

As is his habit, he starts off in Chapter 1 encouraging the Corinthian church and building them up. But by the end of Chapter 2, if you listen closely, you can hear him screaming. I, like so many of you, not only read the bible but I hear it also. So listen with me now and hear what Paul and the Holy Spirit are saying to the church at Corinth and to you and I.

"[1] Paul, called to be an apostle of Christ Jesus by the will of God, and our brother Sosthenes, [2] To the church of God in Corinth, to those sanctified in Christ Jesus and called to be his holy people, together with all those everywhere who call on the name of our Lord Jesus Christ—their Lord and ours: [3] Grace and peace to you from God our Father and the Lord Jesus Christ. [4] I always thank my God for you because of his grace given you in Christ Jesus. [5] For in him you have been enriched in every way—with all kinds of speech and with all knowledge— [6] God thus confirming our testimony about Christ among you. [7] Therefore you do not lack any spiritual gift as you eagerly wait for our Lord Jesus Christ to be revealed. [8] He will also keep you firm to the end, so that you will be blameless on the day of our Lord Jesus Christ. [9] God is faithful, who has called you into fellowship with his Son, Jesus Christ our Lord." I Corinthians 1:1-8

Now, most of us who are teachers can't wait to begin teaching on the truths Paul has already spoken, i.e.: sanctified in Christ; called to be his holy people; grace; gifts, and so on. But I am going to resist this temptation and move on. The message that I want you to see and what I believe will change your understanding of who you are and who you were created to be, follows. Listen with your spiritual ears.

Understand that this book is written to believers. It pictures believers in conflict. In reality, it is a picture of the church of today. It aught not to be this way and Paul sets out to help them (and us) see what is taking place. Hopefully, it helped their understanding as much as it has helped mine. Also, you must see this. Paul has already been there. He has spent time with them, teaching them the gospel and has shared with them the principles of Christian living. So if you hear his frustrations coming out, you will understand where he is coming from.

First off, Paul establishes the understanding that the wisdom of this world cannot compare to the wisdom from the Father. "The foolishness of God is wiser than man's wisdom, and the weakness of God is stronger than man's strength." I Corinthians I:25. Then, he goes on to establish that he did not come to them in great human wisdom. "My message and my preaching were not with wise and persuasive words, but with a demonstration of the Spirit's power, so that your faith might not rest on men's wisdom, but on God's power." Chapter 2:4. Follow along with me as he continues:

Verse 6. "We do, however, speak a message of wisdom among the mature, (*ouch) but not the wisdom of this age or of the rulers of this age, who are coming to nothing." Other translations used the term "natural wisdom" to describe this wisdom to which he is referring. V.7 No, we speak of God's *secret wisdom*, a wisdom that has been hidden and that God destined for our glory before time began."

*(Get the revelation on this. Before time began, God prepared his secret wisdom for us.) Why would Paul mention this if it weren't part of the restoration? Oh, I suppose some would say that we lost this when we fell in the garden. Do you believe God is cruel so he puts it here to show us what we missed out on? No, it is ours in Christ Jesus. Now listen to this:

"[8] None of the rulers of this age understood it, for if they had, they would not have crucified the Lord of glory. [9] However, as it is written: "What no eye has seen, what no ear has heard, and what no human mind has conceived these things God has prepared for those who love him" (*This is for now, not for some time in the future when we are no longer in need of it.)

"[10] for God has revealed them to us by his Spirit. The Spirit searches all things, even the deep things of God. [11] For who knows a person's thoughts except that person's own spirit within? In the same way no one knows the thoughts of God except the Spirit of God. [12] We have not received the spirit of the world but the Spirit who is from God, that we may understand what God has freely given us."

I hope you are reading the same scriptures I am for what it is saying is that we can know what's on the mind of God for us. We have been given His Spirit. Remember, we are the Temple of God and He lives within us. We are the Ark of God. Entrusted in us, are the very words of God. If you can handle it, we are the Holy of Holies where the Ark resides. In us is the manna, the bread of life, which is, of course, Christ Jesus. I know this will stretch some of you, but try to think it through.

"[13] This is what we speak, not in words taught us by human wisdom, but in words taught by the Spirit, explaining spiritual realities with Spirit-taught words. [c] [14] The person without the Spirit does not accept the things that come from the Spirit of God but considers them foolishness, and cannot understand them because they are discerned only through the Spirit. [15] The person with the Spirit makes judgments about all things, but such a person is not subject to merely human judgments, [16] for, "Who has known the mind of the Lord so as to instruct him? But we have the mind of Christ." Who is Christ except God?

This is what we have just read: We have the mind of Christ and the Spirit of God has made known to us His will. His Spirit is attuned to our spirit. We now have access to the mind of the Spirit of God. The secret mysteries of God are ours! Because of this, we should never get caught unaware of the schemes of the enemy for our lives. After all, are we not seated in heavenly places with Christ? Does not Christ hear the schemes that the enemy submits to his Father who He sits next to? Is He not our Lord and do we not hear from Him?

I think I have come to understand Isaiah 55:8-9 in a new way, when it says: "For my thoughts are not your thoughts, neither are your ways my ways, declares the Lord. As the heavens are higher than the earth, so are my ways higher than your ways and my thoughts than your thoughts." This was from the time of the fall and in part the timing for this has now been completed and God is making His thoughts and His will known to us. I am not saying that God's ways are still not higher than ours. Only that He is making His ways know to us.

Was Jesus not our model? John 5:19 tells us that Jesus did only what he sees his Father doing. John 17 tells me that Jesus and the Father are one and that we are one with them. Sons of God we are! (Yoda)

Here is yet another truth about our model. There is a statement in the Bible that is repeated frequently which has always given me much thought. It is this statement: "In Christ." This simple statement, two words has given me years of head scratching. I've spent many hours for many years thinking about what it means and how it applies to our lives. I guess simply it means you can't be saved without being *in Christ* and you can't be *in Christ* without being saved. Wow, I'm a genius! But there is more.

I think the first mention of this principle is in Genesis. It says, "For this reason a man will leave his father and mother and be united to his wife, and they will become one flesh." Genesis 2:24 If we follow this principle into the new testament, Jesus quotes this same verse in Matthew 19:5. and, again, we find it in Mark 10:6. Then Paul in 1 Corinthians 6 puts a little different slant on it in speaking about becoming one with a prostitute. It seems that it is the uniting together that brings about the oneness. But then in verse 17 he takes it one step further. "But he who unites himself with the Lord is one with him in Spirit." Now it is not the flesh that is being united, but the Spirit. We have the right now to be united with Christ Jesus and become one with him and we can see this in John 17.

In this same way, it says in Ephesians 2 and, I hate to give just one verse because all of chapter 2 is on this same subject, but in verse 14 it says, "For he himself is our peace, who has made the two one and has destroyed the barrier, the dividing wall of hostility, by abolishing in his flesh the law with its commandments and regulations. His purpose was to create in himself one new man out of the two." He has brought the Jewish believer and those who are outside of the Jewish faith together in Christ. This has only happened by the blood and body of Jesus our Christ on the cross as the sacrifice for sin. The Bible says that this took place once and for all on that cross.

This same oneness is found throughout Ephesians and in Ephesians 2: 4-5 it says it like this: "But because of his great love for us, God, who is rich in mercy made us alive with Christ even when we were dead in transgressions, it is by grace you have been saved."

Now let's look at Ephesians 5:29-31. The short statement in verse 30 makes a startling declaration, "for we are members of his body." Then again in verse 31 Paul quotes the same Genesis scripture that we began with, "For this reason a man will leave his father and mother and be united to his wife, and the two will become one flesh."

So far we have gone from one with our wives, one with a prostitute, and then one with Christ, and, now again, Paul takes it to we are one with the Church, which is his body. "This is a profound mystery but I am talking about Christ and the church." Ephesians 5:32.

Being one with a prostitute is the same as you and I being one with the world system and not God's.

Go back to Chapter 2 now and read verses 10 and 13. "We were created in Christ Jesus by God to do good works." Then in 13 it says, "But now in Christ Jesus you who once were far away have been brought near through the blood of Christ." We are not only one with our wives, but one with Christ and one with his body, the church. This mystery, which was started in Genesis, Paul brings to light here in Ephesians. We are one with Christ Jesus, which makes us one with the Father and, then, one with each other.

Let me remind you of several verses in John 17. Verse 11, the last part: "Holy Father, protect them by the power of your name the name you gave me so that they may be one as we are one." Verse 20: "My prayer is not for them alone I pray also for those who will believe in me through their message, that all of them may be one, Father, just as you are in me and I am in you. May they also be in us so that they may believe that you have sent me. Verse 22: I have given them the glory that you gave me, that they may be one as we are one. Verse 23: I in them and you in me. May they be brought to complete unity to let the world know that you sent me and have loved them even as you have loved me."

We are back where we were created to be, and the garden is again a beautiful place of fruitfulness where we never have to hide, from our creator God again.

Just as Jesus helps us to define God, the New Testament helps us to define the Old Testament and the principles of God, which are true from beginning to end.

Oneness is a thing to seek after and, when we find it, it should be treated as a treasure of gold. There will never be another divorce where the two are one. One cannot be divided and remain one, so, if you are one with the Father and one with Jesus, then your oneness with each other is assured. Remember, as Christ is one with the Father, we are one in Him. The issue is, do we believe what He says in our Bibles? Why must we go on such journeys? What was the wilderness journey all about?

God took Moses into the wilderness for his own 40 year experience to learn how he could trust God so he could go back and face Pharaoh and bring the children of Israel out of bondage. Then the children of Israel had to go and learn the same lesson. They had to learn how to trust God for themselves before they could go into the battles that they would face in taking the promise land. It was a trust issue.

What's a trust issue? It's a lifestyle of faith in God that He is who He claims to be and that He is going to do what He said He would do. It's been the same issue since creation. Will you trust me? Don't eat of that one tree. You can have it all but that one tree is mine.

Now what is the difference today? We are faced with the same question. The issues of God haven't changed. Will you trust me? You can have it all but you will have to do it by faith. How many of the same mistakes are we going to make? What have we learned so we can face our own battles?

Jesus came to us in the same way as God came to Moses, to set us free from the bondage of unbelief. How many golden calves' will we make? How many times will we refuse the gifts He has provided for us and lust for something more? How many times will we refuse to come back to the garden and eat from His provision? His promise to us is that He will provide everything we need for life and righteousness. I ask you, what more is there?

When God used His finger to write His Word on those stone tablets up on the Mountain in front of Moses, it was not so those 10 commandments would last forever. No, what He was doing was establishing the principle that His word does not change. It is established forever. Carved in stone! All of it, and no matter how hard we try to manipulate it, or make it palatable, it will not be changed. It's as if He was saying, my Word cannot be altered, or changed. I have spoken it and it will last forever. I do not change.

Does this mean that He never changes His mind? No, it means that God is the same yesterday, today and forever. It means that we can count on the fact that what He says one day will be the same the next time. The personhood of our God will always be the same. His written word will never change and everything we want from Him must align with that Word.

Jesus Christ is the stone on which the Word was written so that it could be displayed for all of us to see and He, Christ, modeled it for us so we could see for ourselves how it was to be applied. It came with authority, but it was motivated by love. This love saw the creator of all things, (whether things on earth or things in heaven, things with breath or things established without breath, the one who created everything that was created) hang on a tree for our sins, so you and I could be free, free again to be in right relationship with Him who died and rose again.

Have you ever wondered why the Bible says in 1 Corinthians 11:24 that Jesus says "This is my body which is broken for you," (KJV or Amp.) and, yet it also says, "not one of His bones were broken?"

Now if you can handle this, Jesus was the stone the Ten Commandments were written on. It was a shadow of His death, burial and resurrection. Jesus was the Word of God written on the tablets. These were then broken or destroyed and a new set of tablets had to be made. The first set was made by God, but the second set God made Moses chisel out. God's way or our way? Sounds like the Garden of Eden all over again. We see this played out so many times in scripture. Jericho was God's way, and Ai was man's way. Crucifixion or King? God's way or man's way. Of course, now, on this side of the cross, the words are written on the tablet of our hearts.

Now in Chapter 3:4, Paul's voice really starts to ring out. Not only are they still trapped in human wisdom and reasoning, they are debating with each other over things that in the light of eternity are meaningless. I am of Paul or I am of Apollos. Hear Paul scream, "You don't get it. You are still acting like mere men. You do not understand who you are. You are no longer natural men but God has called you to be sons, His sons or, in other words, you are supernatural men! You have been given God's DNA, so use it. Tap into the Spirit of God and do what He is saying and stop this childish nonsense. You are God's children. Act like it!

I must confess that I still get upset when I hear about some pastor or teacher of the Word being judged by another pastor or teacher or organization. This has gone on forever. Someone gets a revelation or has a teaching and begins to share it and, someone else who hasn't received that revelation and doesn't or can't understand it, starts to criticize it. This new revelation begins to separate them and others from following them and what we have is division in the body. It's almost as if they have said to themselves that if something new is going to come out, it better line up with the way I believe or I'm out of here. As if we, and only we, have the full truth.

Someone falls into sin or hardship and the body of Christ judges them and washes their hands of them. They don't have the bigger picture. They don't understand the fullness of the Lord's prayer in Matthew. "Forgive or I will not forgive."

When I look at the story of the Prodigal Son, I see something so much larger than the story of one rebellious young man coming back home. This is the story of mankind ever since Adam and Eve. It's the story of all of us. Each one of us goes through a time of doubt and questions at sometime in our lives. Each one of us gets weak in our faith when faced with certain things unique to them that seem overwhelming at the time and we run away. Maybe we don't completely leave Him but our faith in Him has taken a big hit. And what does the Father do? He waits and longs for our return. He watches to see our dust on the horizon and then He runs to greet us.

God never quits on us. God never quit on mankind. The core of everything God ever did had the restoration of His creation (mankind) back into relationship to Him, at His heart.

The big picture is that God wants us all restored to Him, yet when we see a mistake or sin in someone, a weakness or fault, we go into judgment on them and cast them out. What ever happened to "restore that one in love"? That Prodigal Son received a whole new inheritance when he returned. Why don't we give that kind of forgiveness to one another?

I'm aware there are exceptions and I know the scriptures which say to separate yourselves and to not fellowship with such a one, but those were written to warn us against those who were not truly believers and who were acting as if they were, those without repentance. The word also comes against those who were teaching another gospel, one that was against the true gospel of Christ. This was not against those believers who fall or get revelations you don't agree with. And don't try that old one on me that if they were really believers, they wouldn't sin. Get real. Look in the mirror sometime after a good fight with your wife or a friend. Would you want everything you said broadcast over the body of Christ shouted from the roof tops!

Judgment is a disease in the body of Christ and it is transmitted just as a common cold, from one mouth to another. We say we forgive but, in fact, we don't. A fallen or mislead leader or pastor is branded forever. We extend partial forgiveness based on their performance and say out of the goodness of our heart that they can be a part of the body of Christ, but never get behind the pulpit again. What's that all about? Partial forgiveness is no forgiveness at all.

Thank you, God, that you didn't or don't forgive like we do. His forgiveness is complete and forever. We, on the other hand, are still trying to extract a penalty, a payment for what we consider to be sin, and we do that according to how grievous the offense was, when, in fact, Jesus already paid the full price for that sin. Do we know better than Him? Did He miss something? When is forgiveness going to really mean forgiveness? When are we going to understand the fallen state of our flesh?

Yes, we are brand new creatures in Christ, but did you notice you still have a body that didn't get that message? We still wrinkle up and die! We seem to have the tendency to major on the scriptures that condemn, and minor on the ones of forgiveness, and yet, without forgiveness, none of us would be around to judge one another.

On His last night, Jesus washed the feet of His disciples including Judas who would betray Him, and yet Jesus knew that within hours they would all abandon Him. Was He wrong about them or were the affects of the cross more complete then we have understood?

Perhaps my arguments here are too simplistic. Well, then, let's move on to the gifts of the Spirit. They are in scripture and encouraged to be used, but they have ripped apart the body of Christ forever. What about healing which was paid for by the stripes on Jesus' back and yet denied by so many for this day and time? It's even taught that sickness can be from God. Is that not a house divided? Or how about personal prophesy or the rapture?That's good enough for a church division.

You can easily understand why there are so many churches or organizations. Each one believes that they have it right on something that the rest of us don't truly understand. So why not go ahead and do it our way and keep the others out of our circle?

You would never guess it by the way some people teach and put on airs, but we are all still under construction. God is not done with any of us who are still breathing. Check yourself. Yes, that does mean you. You breath, you sin. You need a savior. Stop judging others and your life will be much better.

What are you saying, Lord, to me?

So Big, Our God is So Big!

Truly Gods ways are beyond our comprehension.

"Oh, the depth of the riches of the wisdom and knowledge of God! How unsearchable his judgments and his paths beyond tracing out! Who has known the mind of the Lord? Or who has been his counselor? Who has ever given to God, that God should repay him? For from him and through him and to him are all things." Romans 11:33-36

Even though, as we have read in I Cor.1-2, we have the mind of Christ and we can hear the deep and secret things of God. We, in our humanity, cannot grasp the fullness of the Godhead. There will always be more to learn.

As I understand it, if we can see it, feel it or touch it, it cannot contain God. God can be in it, but it cannot contain Him. No matter how great the Hubble Telescope is, it cannot not find the home of

God, or see the fullness of His Kingdom, and yet God dwells within it. Everything we can see or ever will see in our lives on this earth and in the heavens above has been made by His spoken Word.

Think about this: Has it ever crossed your mind what might have been the priorities of God when He created the world? Before He created the Grand Canyon, before He made the seven wonders of the world, before *time was broken out of eternity*, what was on His mind? Before He made the sun and moon and all the starry host, what was on God's heart?

You and I! Mankind! We have this saying, "It's all about Him!" And in it's fullness it is. But creation was all about us! Everything that was ever created was about us. Everything was about us and for us. He made this world, this planet and it's solar system for us to live in and, of course, it's all about His love for His creation. The wonders of God, the love of God, is what is suppose to come forward when people look at us to see Him.

When people look at His creation, they are suppose to see Him. "[20] For since the creation of the world God's invisible qualities — his eternal power and divine nature — have been clearly seen, being understood from what has been made, so that men are without excuse." Romans 1:20

What was in His thinking? I offer you this: "I am going to make an expression of myself and put flesh on it and give it a place to flourish so we can have relationship and so they can relate represent me."

You and I, then, are the most incredible creations He ever made! We were the first priority of God. Can you guess what came next? I believe grace was next or maybe it's the other way around.

[9] who has saved us and called us to a holy life — not because of anything we have done but because of his own purpose and grace. This grace was given us in Christ Jesus *before the beginning of time,* 2 Timothy 1:9. Before we were, before we ever had the opportunity to fall in the garden, to turn from His ways to go our own ways, He gave us grace. Even before He established what we call time He gave us grace which came in the form of Jesus Christ.

What does this mean? It means that the fall, which we took in the garden, was also planned for. Even though we were created perfect, we were given a free will to think for ourselves and, of course, we chose to become self-centered instead of God-centered. This has been a way of life for us ever since then. Eating of the tree of *"Good and Evil"* threw us into humanity instead of Godliness. God knew beforehand that we would be in need, not only of a savior, but a ton of grace to go along with Him. "[4] For he chose us in him before the creation of the world to be holy and blameless in his sight. In love [5] he predestined us to be adopted as his sons through Jesus Christ, in accordance with his pleasure and will — [6] to the praise of his glorious grace, which he has freely given us in the One he loves.

Ephesians 1:4-6

It also means that Jesus was not someone who God gave us because we sinned. He was with the Father from the beginning.

Jesus was not just an emergency plan or plan two because plan one failed. He chose us! Before time, He chose you and I to be in Him. He chose us to be like Him, conformed to His image to be holy and blameless in His sight. From the beginning His plan for us was to be His sons. This all took place by His will and His good pleasure. Beyond that, He gave us grace in the Lord Jesus Christ. This took place before Adam or, for that matter, before the earth were created.

Because of this, I think it is safe to say that if you have ever wondered if God was aware of your needs, let me just say the obvious, yes! If you ever wondered if you were a child of lust and not planned for, let me just say the obvious again, no!

"Yet to all who received him, to those who believed in his name, he gave the right to become children of God, children born not of natural descent, nor of human decision or a husband's will, but born of God." John 1:12-13

There will never be a need in your life that you will have or that you have now, that God does not know about and that He has not worked out for your best and His glory. It may not seem like it now, but it will be revealed to you in His time.

This is not to say that things do not go wrong, but the response for those who are in Christ is already planned for. Every detail, every hair on your head, every breath that you breathe, every path you take, is planned for. "[23] The steps of a good man (other translations say "of a righteous man") are ordered by the LORD: and he delighteth in his way." Psalms 37:23

An illustration that Lord gave me from His word might help us understand this even better. "[19] Therefore, brothers, since we have confidence to enter the Most Holy Place by the blood of Jesus, [20] by a new and living way opened for us through the curtain, that is, his body, [21] and since we have a great priest over the house of God, [22] let us draw near to God with a sincere heart in full assurance of faith, having our hearts sprinkled to cleanse us from a guilty conscience and having our bodies washed with pure water. [23] Let us hold unswervingly to the hope we profess, for he who promised is faithful." Hebrews 10:19-23

The Curtain here is a picture of the Lord Jesus Christ as a gate and a guardian and when He was torn on the cross, at the same moment the Curtain was also torn from top to bottom. The tear was complete and the way was now open for you and I to enter into the Holy of Holies. We now, because of the torn Curtain had access to God. Jesus opened the door and said to come on in and meet My Father. Never again do we have to be afraid of coming into His presence. "[7] Therefore, Jesus said again, "I tell you the truth, I am the gate for the sheep." And, "[9] I am the gate; whoever enters through me will be saved. He will come in and go out, and find pasture." John 10:7,9.

I once had a vision of me entering the throne room of God and I was all the way in the back with my head down shuffling my feet and I felt like I didn't belong there. All of a sudden, as if in a stop action movie, I was zooming through the people and, when I stopped, I was staring at the Lord's feet right in front of me. Then I heard the word that said I was never again to feel as if I didn't belong there. We were designed to be in His presence and we can now enter into the throne room of God with our heads up any time we choose. Up close and personal. We get the front row.

Another picture of Jesus Christ is Israel. Just as Christ was chosen to suffer for His kingdom, Israel was chosen by God, called out by God, to suffer. They were chosen by God to bring forth the redemption of the whole world through His word. Theirs was given to be a life of rejection and condemnation, suffering, fighting the battles, and keeping the Word of God secure from all the enemy's of that Word. Yes, they won some battles, but they have lost more of their people for the righteousness of God than any other people. God, Himself, destroyed some when they chose to sin and some were destroyed by people who wanted to keep God's Word out of our lives. Some were destroyed by those who were jealous of their calling. Can you imagine that?

Jealous of a people called by God to suffer for Him and for preserving His gospel for us.

Israel has foes that will do anything to keep the Word of God from being proven right. Most of the Israelis would be happy if God called someone else to do all the suffering. Millions upon millions of the people of Israel have been slaughtered because of His name and the Word of God.

Another picture of Christ is the church. From the beginning, we, the church, the body of Christ, were designed by God to be the fullness of Christ. "²³ which is his body, the fullness of him who fills everything in every way." Ephesians 1:23 We are to be a picture of Christ, to suffer with Him for the world, to carry our cross, so that, through us, the message of that torn Curtain would go out to all the world. The message is that of the kingdom of God and we are to use the Word of God to bring this message of the love and forgiveness of God for His creation. We, once again, have access to God, which we lost in the garden, through Him being the torn curtain or the torn robe of God.

What do I mean the robe of God? In scripture, a high priest would tear his robe when a blasphemy was committed. Our great High Priest did the same when the greatest blasphemy of all time was committed on the cross. Jesus, the perfect one, the one without blemish or sin, the single sacrifice for all mankind, took on all the sins of mankind and the Father, unable to look at that sin, tore His robes, and the veil was opened.

Here's a thought. The word says that we are seated in the heavenly places with Christ. Is this positional or is it our spirit that is with Him? I have shared this thought with several other teachers of the Word since the Lord dropped it on me. All of them have said "both".

Well, now, this answer presents another set of questions for me. If our spirit is with Him and our spirit is also with us, does that mean our spirit has the ability to be in more than one place at a time? Does it mean that our spirit is already eternal, not restricted by time and place? If this is true, then, are we, our souls, *playing catch up* with our spirit? If our spirit is seated with Christ which is on the right hand of the Father, then we are within earshot of what heaven is talking about. This leads me to the understanding of scripture which says that we should not be caught unawares."[4] But you, brothers, are not in darkness so that this day should surprise you like a thief." I Thessalonians 5:4.

We get the news of his plan before Satan gets his answer from God and we should be able to hinder his plans, instead of the other way around. It says that we are not unaware of the enemy's devices. In other words, we are not unaware of his plans and scams and we should not be caught in these. We should be aware of his plans of evil for us and be able to head them off, cancel them out before he gets a chance to put them into action.

Satan's plans are to keep us from achieving our potential in Christ. In other words, he wants to keep us from becoming everything our God created us to be. Most Christians are living so far beneath their potential that I have called us subterranean Christians. We can achieve so much more.

Vision of the film:

Most Christians are rather like un-developed film negatives. On my way to the drug store to have some film developed, the Lord showed me a picture of what most Christians are like and how they resemble the film I was taking in to be developed. As is, it is just a roll of hope that could hold great promise. As it goes through the first process, there is a shadow that appears (a negative) to show the promise of a beautiful picture. However, it takes the process of development for us to be able to see the real picture. Without development, it is only an unfulfilled promise of what is available.

You and I are born as a package of promise and, with the right care and development, we turn out as a negative that shows a shadow of what we can become in Christ. As we give ourselves to Him, more and more of the dark disappears and the true purpose of our birth comes into clear focus and beauty.

If we give it the right amount of time and allow the process to come to its end, the picture will turn out to be a beautiful representation of Christ. "Christ in us the hope of Glory."

This is new understanding: God said to me that the Temple is the Capital building of the Kingdom of God and that is now located within us. What does the Capital stand for? It is the seat of authority. You and I, representing God on this earth, are the seat of His authority, for we are now the temples of God. This must be proclaimed in all the earth. We are truly the image and likeness of God in Christ Jesus and we have great authority on this earth. We must learn how to proclaim and declare His plans and purpose for mankind.

Related scriptures for your study:

Romans 8:28- Called according to His purposes, not our own.

John 9:4 Jesus says that He must do the work of Him who sent Him.
John 20:21 Says that Jesus is sending us out in the same way that the Father sent Him.
James 2:14-18 Faith vs. Works.
Rev. 2:1-6 Works vs. Relationship- First love.
Gen. 1: 26-27 The garden before the fall

Matt. 25: 34 The Kingdom from the beginning; this, then, is the garden.

Col. 1: 12-13 Qualified by God to share in His Kingdom and brought us into the Kingdom of His Son. The now kingdom
Gal. 5: 22 Eat the fruit in the garden.
Phil. 2: 1-5; Rom.12: 10; Eph. 5: 1; I Cor. 3: 16; I Cor. 6: 19; II Cor. 6: 16

Isn't it always this way? Just about the time when you think you understand God and His Word, at least to some degree, someone gives you another understanding. It happened to me last night but I am going to have to work on this for some time before sharing it. Maybe it's another book.

Truly the world cannot contain Him. He's always larger than we think!

What are you saying, Lord, to me?

The Anointing Breaks the Yoke

I have a friend who years before he became my worship leader he gave me a prophetic word; "You are a yoke breaker". This was years before this became a teaching by those like Cindy Jacobs, Dutch Sheets, and Chuck Pierce. Wonderful teachers all but to be quite honest when it was first spoken to me I had no idea what it meant then nor years later when these prophets and teachers spoke to the church. It was a prophecy and teaching that seemed to just go over my head and land on others who rushed out to buy the latest book on yoke breaking. It left me feeling quite inadequate as a teacher of the word.

As most of us I was raised up and taught that the yoke was like an ox yoke and Jesus and you yoked together in this thing could accomplish anything as long as we stayed hooked together. I don't know how many sermons I taught or how many times I have heard this same thing expressed from enumerable pulpits throughout the years. I even know a church that has a oxen yoke on the wall behind their pulpit. It sounds great, Jesus and you pulling together. Wow, together we could do anything. This is very true but not exactly what is meant by scripture.

Over the past few years the Lord has had Marlene and I studying the Hebraic roots to our Christian belief system and our eyes have been opened to many wonderful truths that have been hidden from us. Not hidden by God but hidden by our New Testament Theology, our Churchianity, and our desire to move away from anything from the Old Testament. We wanted the new not the old and because we refused to understand that the New Testament was in fact the completion of the Old Testament we missed so very much.

A few nights ago I heard something which just blew me away. Our pastor, Anthony Turner was speaking and he mentioned that the bible says that God gave us the anointing to break the yoke. All of a sudden the words I had received so many years before came into focus for me. The fog was gone and I understood. God has called me to be a yoke breaker! Before I simply had no understanding what that truly meant, now there came a knowing, an understanding the lights were turned on, and now along with the knowledge I have gained from studying my Hebrew roots it means everything.

In Matt.11 Jesus makes these statements: [29] Take my yoke upon you and learn from me, for I am gentle and humble in heart, and you will find rest for your souls. [30] For my yoke is easy and my burden is light. Matthew 11:29-30 New International Version - UK (NIVUK)

First off we must put on our Hebrew hats so we can see what this meant in first century Christianity.

Every city or town had multiple Rabbis in it. Every Rabbi had his own view or understanding of what particular scriptures meant and every city or town had children whose fathers had selected a Rabbi who had the views he wanted his sons to be trained in. Most if not all of these were very burdensome as the Pharisees and Sadducees pretty much controlled what the Rabbis taught. There was another book that held as much or more influence as the Torah. This was called the Talmud and it contained the combined views of the most important Rabbis on what the Torah was saying. This is much the same as we study the Commentaries along with the word of God to grasp the meanings of the most difficult passages.

As different as all the Denominations are plus all the independent churches of today the Rabbis all had their own views on the Torah and how it was to be walk out. This was known as the Rabbis yoke.

Jesus was a known Rabbi and of course He had His own views and that is why He said [29] Take my yoke upon you and learn from me, for I am gentle and humble in heart, and you will find rest for your souls. [30] For my yoke is easy and my burden is light.

One of the most obvious differences between Jesus' rabbinical understanding and that of the other Rabbis was that Jesus chose His own pupils to teach they did not choose Him. As we know Jesus chose twelve and they were called His disciples.

A unique thing about disciples is that no matter who their Rabbi was there was a very strong tie to them and the disciples longed to be just like them. It is said that the disciples of Jesus wanted to be so close to Him that as they traveled the roads they would get so close that the dust off the feet of Jesus would get on them. They wanted to act like Him and imitate Him in every thing He did. This is why when Jesus was walking on the water on the Sea of Galilee and Peter saw this; his response was to ask Jesus to bid him to come to Him. His desire was to be just like Jesus.

[25] During the fourth watch of the night Jesus went out to them, walking on the lake. [26] When the disciples saw him walking on the lake, they were terrified. It's a ghost, they said, and cried out in fear. [27] But Jesus immediately said to them: Take courage! It is I. Don't be afraid. [28] Lord, if it's you, Peter replied, tell me to come to you on the water. [29] Come, he said. Then Peter got down out of the boat, walked on the water and came towards Jesus. [30] But when he saw the wind, he was afraid and, beginning to sink, cried out, Lord, save me! [31] Immediately Jesus reached out his hand and caught him. You of little faith, he said, why did you doubt? Matthew 14:25-31 New International Version - UK (NIVUK)

We can see an expression of this today and we call it alignment. We want to be aligned with those who view the outward expression of the word of God as we do. As Paul call on his disciples to imitate him we should do the same today with our leaders who are rightly imitating God.

One of the many things that Jesus had to with His disciples was to overcome the teachings of the Pharisees and Sadducees. I believe that this is why He chose those who flunked out of rabbinical school which all young boys of His day had to attend. The Rabbis would chose the cream of the crop to continue in the more advanced teaching of Torah and those who did not show as much promise would go back to their fathers and take up the family business. Jesus chose from these outcast and misfits to pour into them His life and beliefs. Again this is much like you and I today for the scriptures say:

[27] But God chose the foolish things of the world to shame the wise; God chose the weak things of the world to shame the strong. [28] He chose the lowly things of this world and the despised things— and the things that are not— to nullify the things that are, [29] so that no-one may boast before him. [30] It is because of him that you are in Christ Jesus, who has become for us wisdom from God— that is, our righteousness, holiness and redemption. [31] Therefore, as it is written: Let him who boasts boast in the Lord. 1 Corinthians 1:27-31_New International Version - UK (NIVUK)

Please understand that I in no way want to take the church back to what it was like in the first century. We have had so much ongoing revelation and it will continue to come as long as we make a place for the Holy Spirit to cause us to change and grow.

What my goal today would be is that we would have the body of Christ understand where the New Testament came from and where and what the culture at that time understood it to mean. Our inability to completely understand the Old Testament from a first century perspective has left much to be desired. As we have just seen in this illustration of the yoke we still have much to learn.

So what does all this mean? I know what it means to me and I hope it will be meaningful to you. For me it means setting the captives free. What I mean by that is that there are thousands of Christians who are still being held captive by religion. They are still under the influence of the teachings they had as children or the false teachings of cults or they have just been under the heavy hand of abusive authority and bad teaching about the God who we serve. The world has also been a great teacher only it has lead so many away from the understandings written in the word of God.

The writer of Hebrews says it like this:

[12] For the word of God is living and active. Sharper than any double-edged sword, it penetrates even to dividing soul and spirit, joints and marrow; it judges the thoughts and attitudes of the heart. [13] Nothing in all creation is hidden from God's sight. Everything is uncovered and laid bare before the eyes of him to whom we must give account. Hebrews 4:12-13New International Version - UK (NIVUK)

Paul understood this and in many of the books he wrote he expressed this. [22] You were taught, with regard to your former way of life, to put off your old self, which is being corrupted by its deceitful desires; [23] to be made new in the attitude of your minds; [24] and to put on the new self, created to be like God in true righteousness and holiness. [25] Therefore each of you must put off falsehood and speak truthfully to his neighbor, for we are all members of one body. Ephesians 4:22-24 New International Version - UK (NIVUK)

This for many was a completely different way of thinking. It would mean changing the way you lived and the way you dealt with others. This was going to require a Godly approach which they could only achieve in Christ Jesus. This is why he goes on in Chapter 5:1 and makes this statement: [1] Be imitators of God, therefore, as dearly loved children [2] and live a life of love, just as Christ loved us and gave himself up for us as a fragrant offering and sacrifice to God.

Paul is saying you must put on your new identities and become like Jesus. He was following after Christ teachings as he was breaking off yokes. Get ride of all that old junk that's holding you back and put of the life of Christ. Look to verses 31-32 in chapter 4:

[31] Get rid of all bitterness, rage and anger, brawling and slander, along with every form of malice. [32] Be kind and compassionate to one another, forgiving each other, just as in Christ God forgave you.

I think my first book "Breaking Out of Religious Christianity" was a step in the right direction. If you haven't read it get one and it will help you in your process of becoming free, truly free in Christ Jesus our Lord.

I'm calling all you raised under the heavy hand of religion to come out and be free. He says "come to me for my yoke is easy and my burden is light." Isaiah 58:6 New International Version - UK (NIVUK)

⁶Is not this the kind of fasting I have chosen: to loose the chains of injustice and untie the cords of the yoke, to set the oppressed free and break every yoke? Isaiah 10:27 New International Version - UK (NIVUK)

²⁷ In that day their burden will be lifted from your shoulders, their yoke from your neck; the yoke will be broken because you have grown so fat.

Breaking yokes was something that the prophet Isaiah had an anointing for and so did Jesus and so do you. We are to set captives free whether they are being held captive by sin or the church they need to be free. Don't get the idea that I am against church, I am not. At least not all churches. It's only those who are stuck in the good old days. Those who refuse to grow and truly become like Jesus. We were all made in the image of God to act like Him, look like Him, love like Him in and too this world. That takes on many shapes and sizes. As many people as there are Christians and we still haven't gotten it right. It may take a billion more before we've got the look right because He is soooooo big. So we've got to get to it. He prepared the work for us before He created the earth so before He comes to take it back lets see how many people we can love into His kingdom.

I know that what I am saying is not easy. For many it will mean breaking habits you have had for many years if not all your lives. Some will have to break traditions, family traditions that go way back in your family lines but God is so good that He will help you in this process. He longs to see you look like He created you, not all distorted by sin and lies and He will bring it to pass if you give it to Him.

What are you saying, Lord, to me?

_____

_____

_____

_____

_____

_____

_____

The Return of His Glory

First, we have already seen in Genesis 1:26-28 that we are created in His image and likeness. This includes so much that it would be impossible for me to examine all the aspects of God, not that I would even know them, but within those He includes His Glory. So then, as far as I can see, we are an expression of His glory. How could you have His likeness and be in His image without His glory? Impossible! But so many saints do not believe this. This had to come to me by revelation even though it is in His word in John 17. Jesus is praying to the Father and He says: "Father, I have given them the Glory that you gave to me." We have the Glory of Christ Jesus our Lord which is the glory given him by his Father which is the Glory of God!

Secondly, He said for us to go and be fruitful and increase in number, fill the earth and subdue it. In other words, go and procreate! What is He telling us here? He is telling us to fill the earth with His Glory. Isaiah 6:3 records the Seraphs as saying "Holy, holy, holy is the Lord Almighty; the whole earth is full of His glory." Do you want to see His glory? Reach out and touch a brother or sister in Christ. If they are on fire, then know that the fire in them is the Glory of God that is intended to fill the whole earth.

Many years ago we had a ministry which we called, "Pass it On." This was not the national ministry by the same name. Ours was before that one but I can hear Him again saying pass it on. This time He is not saying pass on all your used goods, but pass on My Glory to all those you come in contact with. It's the light of the glory.

We see, then, that our job description has never, ever changed. He sends us out to fill the earth with His glory. In the New Testament it tells us to go into all the earth and preach the gospel. Well, what is His gospel? His gospel reveals His glory, the glory of God, the Father, and His great love for us. Since God *is* love, then you and I are love, His love to this world. So we are to go out and love this world with His love in us.

What we lost in the garden was His glory (our righteousness) and, for the most part, the understanding of His great love for all of His creation. This has become so obvious for we have spent more time, money, and resources on building things to kill one another then on anything else. Loving one another has just become old, tired words, which have lost the power of their true meaning. Making others more important than ourselves or standing in the gap seems to be covered with cobwebs, lost in the dust of everyday living. We are called to bear one another's burdens. How are we doing? John 17 tells us that Jesus loves us with the same love that His Father gave to Him. Imagine that! This is why the words "Love your neighbor as yourself" have so much meaning. It's a principle which starts with God. It's the same love that the manifested God, Jesus, showed you and I on the cross.

In that John 17 passage we are told that Jesus gave us the glory that the Father had given Him. This is the return of His glory to us that we had lost, or, better said, that we gave up in the garden. We have also been given the Holy Spirit, which is God the Spirit, so again see with me that we have been given that same great love He has for all His creation.

Always remember this, that the Holy Spirit *is God* and cannot be separated out of Him. When we are given the Holy Spirit, we are given all of Him. We, too, are three in one, made in the image of God, Spirit, Soul, and Body. We can compartmentalize these as God did with the Father, God the Son, and God the Holy Spirit, but we cannot separate ourselves from ourselves anymore then God can if we are in Him.

Second Corinthians 5 tells us that we have been given the ministry of reconciliation. We are to bring back from the fall those who He created so that they can again experience His great love for them, and then again the whole earth can be full of His glory.

If you are still questioning how you can do these things, spend some time in I Corinthians 1-3. This tells us that not only do we have the mind of God but that we are expected to be using it so as not to live as mere men. Remember, in the same way that Jesus was both a physical and Spiritual representation of the Father on earth so you and I are also.

His Glory *is* His creation and is in His creation. What does this mean to us? That, my friends, is what you and I are to Him! We are the Glory of God, and our job is to restore people (His creation) to the Glory of Him, the same Glory He created us with in the beginning! Romans 8:30 says this, "Those He justified He also glorified." So much so that He even sends us out to forgive sins in His name. "Receive the Holy Spirit. If you forgive anyone his sins, they are forgiven; if you do not forgive them, they are not forgiven." John 20: 22.

We've been re-glorified! "As a man thinks in his heart, so is he." Proverbs 23: 7.

Again we see in 2 Corinthian 3:18 where it says this, "And we who with unveiled faces, are being transformed into His likeness with *ever-increasing glory*, which comes from the Lord, who is the Spirit." We are being transformed into the likeness of our creator, and the glory is returning to us. It's the same likeness we were created with! Remember, there is a process to this. The more we stay close to Him, the more of Him we will take on. Our positional standing with God is in tact and it's a done deal, but practically we are walking this out step by step.

It all goes back to 2 Samuel 9, the story of David and Mephibosheth. This is a great masterpiece, if you will. It's an oil painting made up of words of the glory returned, painted by the greatest artist of all time. It pictures the return of everything that was lost in the garden, plus it also pictures the wealth of the wicked laid up for the righteous. Mephibosheth is the picture of those who are covered by a covenant. Which is who? That's right, us. We are the children and heirs of this blessed covenant God made with His creation. Read it again. It's a short story with an eternal message.

As we have already seen in 2 Corinthians 5, we are the righteousness of God. We understand from this that the veil has been removed and we are now in right standing with the Father who no longer counts our sins against us (v.19).

Why the unveiled face? Because the Holy Spirit is not on us but in us and we no longer must fear it departing as Moses did, so now the glory of God can once again be seen and spread about the world. It's the opposite of Moses. He had to keep his face covered so the glory of God would not leave. But now we are the Temples of God and His glory is within us, and it is trying to get out of us and fill the earth, so no more veils. Okay? We have the glory of God in us, and it is the glory Christ gave us. If the veil is still on us, then it's a religious veil and not one of relationship. A veil of relationship is a veil of glory and it will not depart from us no matter how many times we fail in our efforts to walk out who we are.

Why are we filled with His glory? So we can now go out and rightly represent Him to the world and win the lost back into a relationship with their maker, the creator of all.

Let me count it down like this. God lives in me. Jesus lives in me. The Holy Spirit lives in me. What of God am I missing? Nothing! I have it all, only now I need the manifestation of these to come forth in every part of my life so I might lead the world to Him. Does this sound good? Well, it has your name and address on it also.

What does this include? His love, His grace, His mercy, His power, all the gifts of the Spirit, His wisdom, His knowledge, His passion, His glory. Every attribute of God is in me. Please see with me that this ushers in the majesty of His creation. Adam was a glorious majestic creation of God, and you need to understand that so are you! Just suppose God wanted to reproduce Himself. What would He do? He made Adam, and you and I are that Adam.

How important are these things for us to understand? Very important, in fact they are vital in every way. Without knowing these truths, we can only act like Him, but when we truly know these truths, then we can represent Him in fact! Jesus came as the second Adam because we messed up the first one. We can't mess this one up. We can miss Him but foul Him up, we can't do.

This morning I am reminded of a vision the Lord gave me some time back and one that I included in my first book Breaking Out Of Religious Christianity. I'll share it again

Vision:

One day I was sitting on my sofa listening to worship and I began to see a vision. At first, I could not see it, because it was very dark, but then there appeared a very small bit of light coming from around what looked like rubble. This all happened as if it were a part of a movie with a director calling for more light and different camera angles. Then a little more light came in, and I could see more clearly. It looked like the Temple Mount, but on the Mount it was just rocks, rubble spread all over the ground. Then, all of a sudden, miraculously, the rocks begin to move, and the temple starts to be reconstructed. It was coming together, but not by the hands of man. Supernaturally, the Temple came together, a Temple not made with human hands.

As this took place, the light began to get brighter and brighter. Again, it's like in a movie, and the camera pulls back and now we could see what was really taking place. The Temple has come together and everything is complete except for the roof. Now the camera angle changes from a front view to an overhead view and you can look right in and see the outer court, the inner court, and the Holy of Holies. More light appeared and once again the camera is pulled back.

Wow! As I look now, I can see that the Temple has been reconstructed in the torso of a very large man. He is transparent and he is lying on the Temple Mount, and the Temple fills his body from the waist to his neck. At this point, the Lord spoke to me saying: *"You are the Temple of God!"* You, just like the Temple, have an outer court (flesh), you have an inner court (soul), and you have a Holy of Holies (spirit). And, of course, to me you are transparent.

As this was being said, it is as if again the camera pulled back and I could see more of the picture. More light shone and back went the camera still more, and now I could see the whole picture.

The man appears to be waking up. As he does, he stretches out his arms and he hits the golden dome on the Temple Mount and knocks it loose. (I am using the word mosque here for lack of a better word to describe it, but, in reality, the mosque is next door and there is even a larger one under ground.) He picks up this mosque and begins to roll it along his arms and behind his neck and over to the other arm. It reminded me of what some basketball players can do with the ball when they're just playing around. Then, as the mosque came back and over to the other arm, I thought it was going to fly off the end of his hand. Just then he wrapped his hand over it and drew it back into the middle of his chest, which is where our Holy of Holies is.

I had trouble understanding this at first, but then the Lord said to me, "I died for all men, and these who are represented by the mosques are also made in my image and likeness." (Since September 11, 2001, this has taken on even more meaning to me.) Then the man began to sit up, and the camera drew back once more. He stood up and began to walk. Up to this point, the entire vision was in black and white except for the dome on the mosque which was gold. Watch with me now as he takes each step, as his heels rise up. I could see beautiful green grass and flowers blooming in brilliant colors and the Lord said to me, "When my people truly understand who I created them to be, they will take life *everywhere* they put their feet!" Wow! This makes "go into the world and preach the gospel" come alive in me.

We now see how God is supernaturally bringing the rubble of the temple, (our lives as individuals and then corporately as the church) back together. He is reconstructing His church and His people. Here we see a picture of the living stones spoken of by Peter and God supernaturally moving us into the right positions. "But now God has placed the members, each one of them, in the body, just as He desired." I Corinthians 12:18 The light, which kept coming, is the Spirit and revelation that is coming to awaken the body.

He is in the process of bringing the rubble of our lives together as the new temple of God, so we, the temples, can go forth as the glory of God into all the earth. Nehemiah used the rubble that was there to rebuild the walls and the temple that had been burned and broken down. This took place amidst great persecution. The rebuilding of our lives go on.

My life and many others are a testimony to the truth that it is never too late; it is not too late to allow God to have His way with our lives. He will make something beautiful, something useful out of each one of them. "And provide for those who grieve in Zion-to bestow on them a crown of beauty instead of ashes, the oil of gladness instead of mourning, and a garment of praise instead of a spirit of despair. They will be called oaks of righteousness, a planting of the Lord for the display of his splendor." Isaiah 61:3

In the reconstruction of the temple, God is giving us what we will need for the coming of the conclusion of this life as we know it on earth. Eternity is just around the corner and we are in a time of preparation for it. We have been given the privilege of helping others in this process of preparation.

My wife was just reading Proverbs 8. It seemed to be a perfect fit for what we will need.

[1] Does not wisdom call out? Does not understanding raise her voice? [2] On the heights along the way, where the paths meet, she takes her stand; [3] beside the gates leading into the city, at the entrances, she cries aloud: [4] "To you, O men, I call out; I raise my voice to all mankind. [5] You who are simple, gain prudence; you who are foolish, gain understanding. [6] Listen, for I have worthy things to say; I open my lips to speak what is right. [7] My mouth speaks what is true, for my lips detest wickedness. [8] All the words of my mouth are just; none of them is crooked or perverse. [9] To the discerning, all of them are right; they are faultless to those who have knowledge. [10] Choose my instruction instead of silver, knowledge rather than choice gold, [11] for wisdom is more precious than rubies, and nothing you desire can compare with her. [12] "I, wisdom, dwell together with prudence; I possess knowledge and discretion. [13] To fear the LORD is to hate

evil; I hate pride and arrogance, evil behavior and perverse speech. [14] Counsel and sound judgment are mine; I have understanding and power. [15] By me kings reign and rulers make laws that are just; [16] by me princes govern, and all nobles who rule on earth. [17] I love those who love me, and those who seek me find me. [18] With me are riches and honor, enduring wealth and prosperity. [19] My fruit is better than fine gold; what I yield surpasses choice silver. [20] I walk in the way of righteousness, along the paths of justice, [21] bestowing wealth on those who love me and making their treasuries full. [22] "The LORD brought me forth as the first of his works, before his deeds of old; [23] I was appointed from eternity, from the beginning, before the world began. [24] When there were no oceans, I was given birth, when there were no springs abounding with water; [25] before the mountains were settled in place, before the hills, I was given birth, [26] before he made the earth or its fields or any of the dust of the world. [27] I was there when he set the heavens in place, when he marked out the horizon on the face of the deep, [28] when he established the clouds above and fixed securely the fountains of the deep, [29] when he gave the sea its boundary so the waters would not overstep his command, and when he marked out the foundations of the earth. [30] Then I was the craftsman at his side. I was filled with delight day after day, rejoicing always in his presence, [31] rejoicing in his whole world and delighting in mankind. [32] "Now then, my sons, listen to me; blessed are those who keep my ways. [33] Listen to my instruction and be wise; do not ignore it. [34] Blessed is the man who listens to me, watching daily at my doors, waiting at my doorway. [35] For whoever finds me finds life and receives favor from the LORD. [36] But whoever fails to find me harms himself; all who hate me love death."

If we follow these instructions, doing our best to make a place for this word of God, we will have a future that will truly cause us to look like Jesus.

What are you saying, Lord, to me?

_____

_____

_____

_____

_____

_____

_____

_____

_____

_____

_____

_____

The Goodness of God

What does the goodness of God or the kindness of God truly mean? Romans 2:4 says, "That the kindness or goodness of God leads us to repentance." Let's look at this for a moment.

How do we call a God good that, by His own power and purpose, destroys nations and drives out those who have lived and have risen up generations in their lands? How is that good? How do we call good those who in Jesus' name, like the Crusaders, slaughtered thousands in the name of God? Isn't possession nine tenths of the law? Is murder from God? How could God's people be so cruel? How do we get goodness out of God?

The first thing we must consider is where do we start with trying to understand this, and, again, I must insist that we start at the beginning. Genesis tells us that, in the beginning, God created the heavens and the earth. Evidently, before that there was nothing. So all we know is that before the earth was formed, there was only God. Now this makes me believe that, if it all started with God, then it must be all about what God wants to build and plant and bring forth on this earth. Same thing goes with you and I. If, in fact, God created you and I, then He must have had a purpose and a plan in doing so. Now let's be sure of this and understand that my logic could be flawed, but, if God made me in His own image and likeness, then He must have wanted me to function much like Him.

He created our minds, both conscious and unconscious, to be like His. He gave us feelings and emotions like His and He gave us a free will to use all of His creation in accordance to His will for us. Love was never intended to be an option for it is apart of who He is, so it was included in our make up.

He made angels to do His bidding and give them a free will. They were designed to glorify Him and so were we, but we have never had to. This is where the problem lies. The problem is on our side. We have chosen to not go along with His plan and purpose and, in fact, it didn't take too long for us to turn our backs on it altogether.

Deception came along and we bought into it. It was an investment that has kept giving and giving to the point where the interest has compounded daily. My generation found this out when our children told us that God was dead. Although we had been acting like this, it was never defined quite so clearly before. We had discovered that free will meant that we could do it our way, and what a mess this has brought to all of creation. The destruction of the world began when we decided we didn't want to eat only what He provided for us, fruit and veggies, we wanted meat. Meat meant fire and the energy crisis began. Cutting down the trees He gave us for protection and food, all to feed the fires. More wood for more fires!

Doing it our way has only brought about disaster. Don't get the idea that I'm a tree hugger. I live in a house built out of wood like most of us and I eat meat and so on. But it is not the way it was supposed to be from the beginning.

In the beginning, our job was to take the garden out to the rest of the world but, instead, we took deception and hate. Cain and Abel brought death and war. Now it is almost impossible for anyone of the nations on earth to live next door to one another.

What was God doing all this time? He began by cleansing the world. Whether this happened once or twice, (consider the Gap theory) it did happen. The flood brought us a new chance to try it His way again. But our free will again said no. We know what is best for our lives, so leave us alone. Again and again He brought people into our lives with the message "Do it my way and you will live." So we ignored them, or worst, we killed them so we could go on destroying our lives with His gift of our free will.

So again, I say, what was God doing all this time? He sat up a plan of reconciliation for us. He gave us a blood sacrifice which would pave the way once and forever so we could live as we were created to live, in relationship with Him. You know the story; we had to kill Him so we could take advantage of His blood for the forgiveness of our sins.

I thank God for His blood and the blood of Jesus. But it would seem as through we are acting more like dogs chasing their own tails, circle after circle, doing the same things over and over again and never learning from it. We spill blood all over the earth and still rely on His blood for forgiveness. We are caught up in the fear or flight syndrome, and we are still bringing our swords to the foot washing. We just don't understand the cross or the pure extravagant love for us that it took for Jesus to hang there.

In a meeting, recently, this thought came to me, "Do you truly believe that God would give authority and dominion over creation as it says in Gen. 1:26-27 to those who are not worthy of this calling?" The obvious answer from this desk would be, "No Way". Then it would appear that God seems to have more faith in us then we have faith in Him. In fact, if He is who He says He is and knows the beginning from the end, then this statement is very evident! He did this (gave to us this outpost of heaven called earth to rule in His name) before the fall, but He knew the fall was coming. Now, that is what I would call faith.

Today, most of us know that understanding the Father's love is somehow connected to how we were treated by our earthly fathers. Many of us didn't even know our fathers. If we did have an at home father, chances are he was too busy or too tired to relate with us, so our view of God, the Father, and His love for us could and, in most cases is, tarnished from the get go.

How do I communicate the truth that this is all about the Father and not about the human person of Jesus but about God the Son, God the Holy Spirit and God the Father? Albeit the humanity of Jesus is of the utmost importance to us for, without it, we could not be saved and live eternally with the Father for we would not have had the correct sacrifice. Also, we would not have His recorded Word or His awesome model to live by.

We have spent countless hours teaching about the person of Jesus without understanding that He was the seed of God, the Father, planted in the Virgin Mary. Mary then brought forth the manifested seed of God, Jesus the Christ, who then gave up Himself as payment for our sins on the cross. Yes, there was the humanness of Mary in Jesus and we can praise and bless that person, but who was Jesus? *God* the Son, or maybe we could say *God* in the form of a human. Yes, I know we must see both sides of Jesus to better understand the Christ and the examples He gave us to follow. But not at the expense of the Father who many people set aside, or see Him as the bad guy and Jesus as their friend. We must remember that it is the Father who has, ever since the fall of man, desired to be back in relationship with His creation. He paved the way and He gave of Himself in the person of Jesus so this could take place.

At the same time, it is this very humanness of Jesus that gives us hope that we, too, have the power over death. Not that we won't die, but that we, too, will be raised from the dead as Christ was and that we are also seated with Him at the right hand of the Father.

Jesus is to be glorified the most because He came to represent the Father in the flesh and gave us the example of how we can also do the same. The humanness of Jesus, His soul, had to agree with the plans of the Godhead and be willing to be the sacrifice for us. But, even in this, we see the truth that if He is our example or model then we also can command the soul to obey the plans of God.

Let us never forget that it is only in the person of Christ that we can obtain to the righteousness of God. Jesus is the mediator of the new covenant. He is our Lord and Savior and God in the flesh. We must also remember that Jesus is not only the manifested seed of God, but that He is the Word of God made flesh. So in our attempt to bring the Father back into a place of honor, we cannot forget who Jesus the Christ is or to give Him the honor and respect He most deservedly has.

Without understanding what we call the trinity and all it represents (the one true God), we tend to lose who the Holy Spirit and the Father truly are. All we see is Jesus.

Okay, put your rocks down. As you can see, I have no intent of trying to take anything away from Jesus who gave up His life so we could have true life, but He is the one who has said, "If you see me, you have seen the Father." It is this God we know as Father, Son, and Holy Spirit, and it is He who in one manifested form or another has done everything to right the wrongs we have done and bring us back to Him.

This said, can we now go back and see that there has always been in the heart of God a deep abiding love for us and for us to live this life out according to His plan and purpose? Truly, I say to you, that it is the goodness of God that leads us to repentance, which means that we finally have decided by our own free will to do it His way.

Hannah, our tour guide for our first trip to Israel, asked me if I would do our communion service for the last meeting before we left. I look so forward to going to Israel again. This time instead of just seeing the sights, I want to experience Jesus. I want to sit in the garden and hear the voice of God. I want the revelation of His heart for us, and what it cost Him to give it to us again.

As I set thinking about it, I got a revelation on Luke 22:15. Knowledge is wonderful but, when it comes with revelation, it sets me on fire. Verse 15 says this, "I have eagerly desired to eat this Passover with you before I suffer." Did it ever strike you as funny (not literally funny) that Jesus would eagerly desire to do this right before He was to die the most excruciating death of the cross? Why not put it off for another year or so? That this was something He was looking forward to knowing that it meant He was about to suffer the cross. To me, this speaks volumes about His love. We know He was focused on the cross at this time. We have the account of His travail in the garden. We know He wasn't looking forward to the pain and death that was just hours away. So what was He looking forward to?

Jesus was looking forward to the unrestricted relationship that the Father would now have with His creation. He was looking forward to the restoration of fellowship as the Father, with those He had created and what the cross and His suffering on it would bring.

Vision:

I recently had a vision of the upper room and the last supper. This vision had a different flavor to it then most sermons that have been preached about this occasion. I saw a moving picture of Jesus entering the upper room and His continence was very different then you would expect. Jesus was very excited, almost to the point that He was gitty. As He spoke to His disciples, He was saying, "How I have longed for this time. I have had to wait thousands of years to release to you this new covenant." We read in the word, that for the joy set before him, he endured the cross. This is what He had come for, a new deal with eternal consequences. For Him, this was a party, one He had been waiting for before the creation of the world.

Wow! Does that talk about the Father's desire to be with us or not! If we could only get this! He loves us so much more than we can understand.

And what was this message that we were to receive at the cross?

Tag, your it! Three words which describe the message of the cross. Yes, I will admit to the simplistic view of this statement and I grant you that the message of the cross has much, much fuller meaning but give me some grace and walk with me for a few minutes on this. You see, all that the cross means, all that our minds can understand about the fullness of the cross, would be of little effect if we don't get this part of the message. He died so we could be reunited with the Father, meaning back in right relationship with our creator. And, our purpose in this is so we could do the Father's will.

When Jesus was on the cross and he was close to the end of his earthly life, he made a statement which most of the body of Christ still doesn't understand and, if they do, they sure don't act like it. What he said was this, " It is finished." Most people that I have heard preach on this think he was speaking about his life on earth or the work he came to do was finished. But, that is just part of the message. I believe there is much more to it than that.

What I believe he was saying was more along the lines of this: My job on this earth is over so now it's your turn to take what I have imparted to you and run with it. My purpose in coming to earth as one of you has now been completed, and it is time for me to go so the Spirit of God can come and help you. Or in simpler terms: Everywhere you go, I will be with you. My Spirit will council you and direct you. My Spirit will comfort you and remind you whose you are. Tag, your it. Now, it's your turn to represent Me and the Father here on earth while I go to the Father's side and represent you up there. Go in my name and represent me to the entire world. Preach my kingdom come, my will be done, and I will follow after you with signs and wonders. Prove my word is truth in action. I, in you, and you, in me. This will make a great team. Just like "I and the Father are one" so I, in you, and you, in me, will be one. It's the Father's plan so that all of mankind can be reunited with him.

What are you saying, Lord, to me?

He died so we could be reunited with the Father, meaning back in right relationship with our creator. And our purpose in this so we could do the Fathers Will

This Thing Called Faith

W hat do God, Abel, Enoch, Noah, Abraham, Isaac, Jacob, Joseph, Moses, Rahab, Isaiah, Jeremiah, Ezekiel, Daniel, Hosea, Joel, Amos, Obadiah, Jonah, Micah, Nahum, Habakkuk, Zephaniah, Haggai, Zechariah, and Malachi, have in common? Each one had to risk everything and do what could only be accomplished by faith. Each one is listed in the hall of fame of faith in the book of Hebrews. Each one responded to a call from God to go and do something extraordinary for Him.

Now, some found this more difficult then others, (lions' den, belly of a whale, sawed in half alive) you know the normal kind of stuff that happens when God tells you to do something for Him, but, in the end, they all obeyed Him and did what He asked.

I find this very exciting for what some were asked to do was impossible for man to do. They had to trust that, if what they heard from God was going to take place, then it would take God's interac-

175

tion with them to bring it to pass. Imagine if you can, the one true God, the supernatural, all mighty God, working hand and hand with you to carry out His plans on earth through you. As we commit our hearts to looking at the roots of our belief systems, I believe faith is in a category all by itself.

Without faith we are left to our own abilities and strengths, to get things done. Without faith we are lost for it takes faith to believe that there is a God and more faith to believe that He wants to interact with us, because He loves us. Without faith, this God who we want to be real and who we must believe in for our eternal salvation, says (in the Bible which we must have faith to believe is the Word of God), "Without faith it is impossible to please me." Everything we are told in this Bible and everything we receive from God has to be received by faith. There is no other option.

We cannot believe without faith and we must have faith to believe. This is a real problem and one we must face by faith daily, hourly, minute by minute. Without faith, we are doomed and are regulated to a life without God. We become those unbelievers, those doomed to hell, which is complete separation from God and much more.

So then the question is where do we get this thing called faith, which, we cannot have without faith? Can we buy it or grow it, can we trade for it, can we make it up, is it the same as hope? I know I can have hope without faith. Is that it?

How, if we don't have faith to believe that there is such a thing as faith, can we come up with faith? Have you ever really thought about it? Well, it seems that this God, which we must have faith to believe in, knew that we were going to be in deep trouble if He didn't do something to help this faith thing come forth in us. So when He was designing His image and likeness, He stuck this very elusive thing He calls faith in us.

Romans 12: 3 says this, "³For by the grace given me I say to every one of you: Do not think of yourself more highly than you ought, but rather think of yourself with sober judgment, in accordance with the measure of faith God has given you." God has given you a measure of faith!!

So that's where it came from! Did it come when we believed? No! We had to have it to believe. It's a wonderful, marvelous gift from God. Did you ever wonder where you got the faith to believe in God? Did He give it to all believers? No! He gave it to all of His human creation!!!! Everyone who He made in His image and likeness got it, and that is everyone on earth. No one was left out. You see, this is why we can believe. He, in His great love for us, gave us the faith we would need to believe that there is a higher purpose to us being here.

I know, I know, the next question is what is faith? Hebrews gives us a definition. It says that it is substance of things hoped for and evidence of things not seen.

Ok? Everyone got that?

What kind of definition is that, God? Truth is that God's definition for faith is in the application of it, not in the title.

Let's read this 11th chapter of Hebrews and see what God calls faith.

"[1] Now faith is being sure of what we hope for and certain of what we do not see. [2] This is what the ancients were commended for. [3] By faith we understand that the universe was formed at God's command, so that what is seen was not made out of what was visible. [4] By faith Abel brought God a better offering than Cain did. (Application) By faith he was commended as righteous, when God spoke well of his offerings. And by faith Abel still speaks, even though he is dead. [5] By faith Enoch was taken from this life, so that he did not experience death: "He could not be found, because God had taken him away." For before he was taken, he was commended as one who pleased God. (Application) [6] And without faith it is impossible to please God, because anyone who comes to him must believe that he exists and that he rewards those who earnestly seek him. [7] By faith Noah, when warned about things not yet seen, in holy fear built an ark to save his family. (Application) By his faith he condemned the world and became heir of the righteousness that is in keeping with faith. [8] By faith Abraham, when called to go to a place he would later receive as his inheritance, obeyed and went, even though he did not know where he was going. (Application) [9] By faith he made his home in the Promised Land like a stranger in a foreign country; he lived in tents, as did Isaac and Jacob, who were heirs with him of the same promise. [10] For he was looking forward to the city with foundations, whose architect and builder is God. [11] And by faith even Sarah, who was past childbearing age, was enabled to bear children because she considered him faithful who had made the promise. (Application) [12] And so from this one man, and he as good as dead, came descendants as numerous as the stars in the sky and as countless as the sand on the seashore. [13] All these people were still living by faith when they died. They did not receive the things promised; they only saw them and welcomed them from a distance, admitting that they were foreigners and strangers on earth. [14] People who say such things show that they are looking for a country of their own. [15] If they had been thinking of the country they had left, they would have had opportunity to return. [16] Instead, they were longing for a better country—a heavenly one. Therefore God is not ashamed to be called their God, for he has prepared a city for them. [17] By faith Abraham, when God tested him, offered Isaac as a sacrifice. He who had embraced the promises was about to sacrifice his one and only son, [18] even though God had said to him, "It is through Isaac that your offspring will be reckoned." (Application) [19] Abraham reasoned that God could even raise the dead, and so in a manner of speaking he did receive Isaac back from death. [20] By faith Isaac blessed Jacob and Esau in regard to their future. [21] By faith Jacob, when he was dying, blessed each of Joseph's sons, and worshiped as he leaned on the top of his staff. [22] By faith Joseph, when his end was near, spoke about the exodus of the Israelites from Egypt and gave instructions concerning the burial of his bones. (Application) [23] By faith Moses' parents hid him for three months after he was born, because they saw he was no ordinary child, and they were not afraid of the king's edict. (Application) [24] By faith Moses, when he had grown up, refused to be known as the son of Pharaoh's daughter. [25] He chose to be mistreated along with the people of God rather than to enjoy the fleeting pleasures of sin. [26] He regarded disgrace for the sake of Christ as of greater value than the treasures of Egypt, because he was looking ahead to his reward. (Application) [27] By faith he left Egypt, not fearing the king's anger; he persevered because he saw him who is invisible. [28] By faith he kept the Passover and the application of blood, so that the destroyer of the firstborn would not touch the firstborn of Israel. (Application) [29] By faith the people passed through the Red Sea as on dry land; but when the Egyptians tried to do so, they were drowned. (Application) [30] By faith the walls of Jericho fell, after the army had marched around them for seven days. [31] By faith the prostitute Rahab, because she welcomed the spies, was not killed with those who were disobedient. (Application) [32] And what more shall I say? I do not have time to tell about Gideon, Barak, Samson and Jephthah, about David and Samuel and the prophets, [33] who through faith conquered kingdoms, administered justice, and gained what was promised; who shut the mouths of lions, ³⁴ quenched the fury of the flames, and escaped the edge of the sword; whose weakness was turned to strength; and who became powerful in battle and routed foreign armies. ³⁵ Women received back their dead, raised to life again. There were others who were tortured, refusing to be released so that they might gain an even better resurrection. ³⁶ Some faced jeers and flogging, and even chains and imprisonment. ³⁷ They were put to death by stoning; ^[g] they were sawed in two; they were killed by the sword. They went about in sheepskins and goatskins, destitute, persecuted and mistreated— ³⁸ the world was not worthy of them. They wandered in deserts and mountains, and in caves and holes in the ground. ³⁹ These were all commended for their faith, yet none of them received what had been promised. ⁴⁰ God had planned something better for us so that only together with us would they be made perfect." Hebrews 11:1-40

Did you notice how Jewish this thing called faith is? Almost every one of God's examples given here is Jewish. So then only Jews can have faith, right? No, but this root is the foundation of faith which He wants us to understand. By faith, we must believe that God made Adam and Eve and all of mankind came from them. By faith, we understand that mankind did not crawl out of the ocean as some slimy ooze and build a house to raise our (squid) families in.

When Marlene and I first began serving the Lord together, people said we were people of faith. Fact is we were broke and had no choice. I had just changed salons and much of my clientele didn't follow me all the way across town. I changed shops to be closer to the church and eventually I went to work part-time there. So I worked at the hair salon and the church, and we still had a difficult time.

We came into this marriage with a whole lot of unsettled stuff. We were both in our thirties and had a lot of time to collect things. Bills seemed to come to us as if we were magnetized just to attract them and I don't mean the kind with faces on them. Then, there were those times I remember when there would be a knock on the door and, when we opened it, no one would be there. Instead of a person, there would be bags of food. Blessings after blessings came our way.

God was so faithful to us. That's faith-full. We never had a lot of money, but God never let us go hungry. We've gotten down to peanut butter and crackers a few times but we have never been on the street. Being the pastors' of small churches has never been the way to make lots of money, but I wouldn't change what we've done or where we have been for anything. Many times the offerings were short of our needs but God has always been our source. I don't want to say we live *on* faith but saying we live *by* faith seems somewhat easier to say. Serving a God who has never failed you gives you hope and hope is the substance of things .....well, you know.

Had we known back then what we are discovering now, I don't think things would have been so difficult but, on the other hand, we would not have had the opportunity to learn to trust the Lord the way we do now. As has been said by someone, we don't know the future but we know who holds the future. And, in reality, that's enough for me.

My faith is still in the process of being perfected by God, "Let us fix our eyes on Him not only does our faith grow Jesus, the author and perfecter of our faith," Hebrews 12:2. It would appear that the Bible teaches us that our faith can grow beyond the measure we were given. "Night and day we pray most earnestly that we may see you again and supply what is lacking in your faith," 1 Thessalonians 3:10. And, again, it says, "We ought always to thank God for you, brothers, and rightly so, because your faith is growing more and more, and the love every one of you has for each other is increasing," 2 Thessalonians 1:3. God wants us to continue in the process of being conformed, changed into His Image and Likeness. I am committed to allowing Christ to have His perfect work completed in me. This is both joyful and sometimes painful.

Sometimes I find my mind saying to me, you shouldn't say that. Do you remember the last part of Hebrews 11? But I want His will and so I say to myself, shut up! Grow up and grow on.

As I was thinking about the Lord this morning I began to ask myself who did people think He was while He was here on earth? Some believed Jesus was a savior. Some believed He was the coming king who would set them free from the Roman tyranny.

Some believed Him to be a prophet and that He would rule all of Israel as the prophets of old.

None of them had the larger picture. None of them had a global view that He was the Savior of the entire world. Not even His own disciples. Many of those who followed Him did not believe at all, but there was one woman who did believe.

My account:

In a time when women were no more than slaves to their husbands and seldom far from home, one woman believed what she had heard about Jesus and that was He was a healer. His claim was that He was the Son of the most high God. That He was Immanuel, God with us.

Most likely this woman had never seen Him as she was a social outcast, called unclean by Jewish Law, and she was restricted to her home or at the least from coming into contact with other people. Yet she had heard the teachings about the Messiah since she was a very little girl. She knew the teachings about the tassels on the talit as we call them today. She was aware of what they stood for and that it contained all the law and promises of God. She knew that all the men including Jesus wore these as it was prescribed in the law, and she knew that Jesus was a Torah observing Jew.

This woman knew that if Jesus were whom He claimed to be, that it would be worth the risk of being stoned or even killed for the chance of being healed. This was her time and she was not going to let it escape. Twelve years with this curse was all she could take, and she would rather die than live with it any longer. She would risk it all for this one chance to touch Jesus.

She must have a well thought out plan so she could be in the right place at the time Jesus would be there and to be close enough to get to Him before anyone knew what was happening. She could hear the commotion when He was in the city and this would be her signal. All the followers would be shouting, some in worship, some condemning, and others just watching to see what He would do next.

The streets were full of men, woman and children, spectators and naysayers, and there was much confusion surrounding the scene as they came past. She knew she had to seize this opportunity, push back the fear and make her move. She would not have time to be subtle or sneaky. Best way was to push her way right in, most likely low and on her knees so as to not be stopped.

Fortunately, the street here was narrow and she won't have to go far to get to Him. She hides herself as best she can along the side of the street among the trash and baskets, wagons and all the things we have garages for now. There He is! Now's the time to make her move, keep low, stay out of the way of all the pushing and shoving. The crowd could not stop her, not all the dirt in the street or the feet kicking at her as she pushed herself forward. There's the tassel! Now grab it and hold on!

The Biblical Account:

"²¹ When Jesus had again crossed over by boat to the other side of the lake, a large crowd gathered around him while he was by the lake. ²² Then one of the synagogue rulers, named Jairus, came there. Seeing Jesus, he fell at his feet ²³ and pleaded earnestly with him, "My little daughter is dying. Please come and put your hands on her so that she will be healed and live." ²⁴ So Jesus went with him. A large crowd followed and pressed around him. ²⁵ And a woman was there who had been subject to bleeding for twelve years. ²⁶ She had suffered a great deal under the care of many doctors and had spent all she had, yet instead of getting better she grew worse. ²⁷ When she heard about Jesus, she came up behind him in the crowd and touched his cloak, (many manuscripts say the hem of his garment and this is very important because the garment spoken of was His talit) ²⁸ because she thought, "If I just touch his clothes, I will be healed." ²⁹ Immediately her bleeding stopped and she felt in her body that she was freed from her suffering. ³⁰ At once Jesus realized that power had gone out from him. He turned around in the crowd and asked, "Who touched my clothes?" ³¹ "You see the people crowding against you," his disciples answered, "and yet you can ask, 'Who touched me?' ³² But Jesus kept looking around to see who had done it. ³³ Then the woman, knowing what had happened to her, came and fell at his feet and, trembling with fear, told him the whole truth. ³⁴ He said to her, "Daughter, your faith has healed you. Go in peace and be freed from your suffering." Mark 5:21-34

Jesus had recognized that from somewhere deep inside of this woman she had faith to come as a daughter and not as a slave. The promise of God was for His children, sons and daughters. Remember when Jesus had just been resurrected and Mary wanted to touch Him? Jesus said to her, "I must go to my Father and your Father." With Him, it's all about family.

Can you hear her scream for joy? "He is Messiah!" I'm healed, I'm healed and I am free. I have my life back and I know what I'm going to do with it. I will serve Him all the days I have left.

Seeing is truly believing, but faith is believing before you can see it.

This is an awesome expression of faith. Here we have a Hebrew woman who was not a disciple of Jesus but someone who believed that He was a healer and that power was coming from Him to heal people. She had only heard about this but had not seen it personally. At least it is not recorded in the word.

This is an example of the faith that is in all of us. It's what God put in us when we were created. She never had time before this for her faith to grow or develop her into a mighty woman of faith and power or, for that matter, for her belief in Jesus to grow. It was just raw faith and determination. God and you working together. His gift and your determination.

"Now faith is," we have it! It's not a payment plan, it's a gift. You don't earn it, you've got it.

How can we go through this life with all of its challenges and not exercise faith? What a waste of a good gift. Determination alone never did anything for this woman. She did everything she knew how to do for twelve years and only got worse. But faith found a way to bring wholeness. She may not have believed in Jesus as God the Son before but how do you think she felt afterwards? She placed her very life in His hands. This is faith, the thing hoped for but not yet seen with the natural eye. She must have imagined what living in good health would be like.

I am inserting here an understanding that many of you may never have thought of. I am going to use the term "imagination" and it is not a sin. Think about this. How many of us have ever hoped for something without seeing it in our imagination? Of course I am referring to a Godly imagination. If we are to pray in faith believing for what is hoped for, can we do this without imagining what that would look like? God has given us our imagination. Use it to help define what you are hoping for. It can only build your faith.

Because faith is the evidence of things not seen (in the natural), we need to look at another example of faith walked out. I have found that the second chapter of Mark is a very good example for us to learn from.

Most of you already know this story in Mark 2 but, hopefully, I can shed more light on it for you. It starts as Jesus returns to the town of Capernaum where He had been a few days earlier and the place where He had done so many healings. He had been forced to leave so He could continue to do His work. Now He returns and finds the people will not leave Him alone. He is in a home and it is overcrowded to the point that no one can even get close to the house.

" ¹A few days later, when Jesus again entered Capernaum, the people heard that he had come home. ²So many gathered that there was no room left, not even outside the door, and he preached the word to them. ³Some men came, bringing to him a paralytic, carried by four of them. ⁴Since they could not get him to Jesus because of the crowd, they made an opening in the roof above Jesus and, after digging through it, lowered the mat the paralyzed man was lying on. ⁵When Jesus saw their faith, he said to the paralytic, "Son, your sins are forgiven." Mark 2:1-5

Now see with me:

1. Faith has a clear goal. Verse 3. They knew what they wanted to accomplish and they were committed to see it through.

2. Faith goes out of its way. Verse 4. Since there was no other way to get the job done, they chose an alternate way. They imagined what they were about to do.

3. Faith defies logic. Verse 4. Logic would say that He is so busy that we won't bother Him now and we will come back some other time.

4. Faith won't be discouraged by what it sees. Verse 4. They made a decision to not let anything stand in their way.

5. Faith never gives up. Verse 4. We've gone this far so we are not giving up now.

6. Faith is belief in action. Verse 5. Their faith pays off for their friend and Jesus sees it.

7. If you can do it in the natural, then you don't need faith. In the natural, there was no way this could be accomplished at this time.

These men must have really loved their friend to be willing to go to such extremes as to tear up their neighbor's roof, but it still required faith to do it. They had hope and faith before it could be done. Hope that they could carry it off and faith, that once they did, Jesus would heal their friend.

So then we see here two separate examples of faith, one carried out by a desperate woman and the other carried out by friends of a desperate man.

Lord, help us to be desperate enough to do whatever is necessary to get to you so you can do whatever it is we need in our lives. Help us to exercise this gift of faith you have given us so that we can be vessels that please you. As we have seen in your Word, it takes faith to please God and we want to do just that. Again I quote, "And without faith it is impossible to please God, because anyone who comes to him must believe that he exists and that he rewards those who earnestly seek him." Hebrews 11:6

Let me make sure that you do not misinterpret what I have written. We are loved and accepted and we already please our Lord. If you have accepted the free gift of salvation in Christ Jesus then you are not only pleasing in His sight but you are now apart of the family of God. We are sons and daughters of God! However, there are things that please Him just as there are things that please us. Where did we get it from? Him!

I'm going to pose a question to you that I want you to think about. How can we imitate God if we are still wearing servants' robes? You are a son and, as such, everything the Father has, has been made available to you. We are all called to serve in one capacity or another, but most of us have not been made aware of the joy of being a son and receiving all the blessings He has for His kids.

Remember again the prodigal, he wanted to come back as a servant but his father would not even hear his argument. The father restored to him his sonship and, as such, he was once again heir to the family inheritance. It's all about the family business. So are we. The servant's heart as a son comes when we are able to lay aside our Royal Kingly robes for a time and serve one another. This is what Jesus did when He washed the disciples feet. He never gave up who He was but He laid it aside for a moment as an example for us to follow. We are priests and kings as we have been made family. We do not have to apologize for being joint heirs with Christ. It's who we are. Be happy about it and enjoy all the rights and privileges it gives to us.

You, Lord, have bought back for us the right to live in our true identities. We have been given the privilege to be who you made us from the very beginning. We are Adam, made in your image and likeness.

What are you saying, Lord, to me?

_____

_____

_____

_____

_____

_____

_____

_____

_____

_____

_____

_____

_____

17

Go Ye

W hen the Bible uses the words "Go ye", what does it truly mean? First thing we see is that the word *"go"* is not a suggestion or just a good idea but, it is a *command* from God! Go! However, this does not mean run! Over the years there have been many times that we have run when we received the word go. Often we run ahead and try in our own flesh to do something that we think God is saying. Only to find out down the road it was truly us looking for something to make us feel good or needed ourselves. Other times we have run away from what we were afraid God was saying because we felt inadequate for the call or we were simply fearful of failure. Another view is that running whether to or from, does not give you the mindset to listen carefully for His instruction.

When God says go, this go must become a mindset. Remember, when the Bible said that Jesus *set* his mind to *go*, and, then again, it says the same thing about Paul. Do you think maybe Jesus had to set His mind in order to *go* to the cross? Or Paul, when knowing full well what was waiting for him in Jerusalem could have kept going without setting his mind to the task? Neither one ran towards the call to go, but each took time to pray and consider the consequences. They set their minds to be obedient and, then, took time to listen. So from where I sit, I see it as a commission from God.

As an artist I understand the term commission as when someone hires me to create a picture for them. Payment is expected. With God, payment comes with the joy of helping others to come into a right relationship with the living God. And, of course, "God supplies all our needs according to his riches in glory in Christ Jesus," Philippians 4:13. So, then, when God tells us to go, we are receiving a commission from Him to go, but we still must seek the 'when and where' and many times the 'how' to get the job done right. Running ahead always gets us in trouble. God has set a timing for everything and that timing is critical for us if we want to be in the right place when Jesus returns. We can learn this by looking at Genesis. God came looking for Adam and He was not where He should have been. Where was he? Hiding in the bushes. He was no longer doing what God had created him to do, caring for his wife and the garden. It cost him and all of us dearly.

The plan and purpose God has for us is the very best thing for our lives. Remember the cloud during the day and the fire at night? God moved them when He was ready for them to be moved. Wait, wait, and wait for God. Stay planted until He moves you and be ready to go when He says go. He made you, created your destiny and knows what's best for you. His timing is perfect. I am going to use this story from my own life as an illustration of the timing of God.

While we were in Northern California, I had a job driving a truck for a vending machine company owned by a pastor friend of mine. On my route was a Bank of America in Sonoma, California. The stop before it was at a rest home and, on this particular day when I arrived, there were ants all over the machine and in all the candy. Normally it would take me at the most 10 minutes at this stop to fill the machines and clean up but, on this day, it would take me about 45 minutes. As soon as I was finished and had the manager inspect the break room, we (Marlene was with me and helped me on the truck) were off to the next stop. It was about a 20 minute drive to Sonoma from Petaluma and, as I approached the bank, I ran into a police roadblock.

When I came up to the officer at the roadblock, he asked me where I was going and I said to the Bank of America. He said "not today you're not." I asked what was going on and he told me that there had been a shootout in the bank parking lot and a gunman shot and killed an armored truck guard during a robbery attempt. Then the driver of the armored truck got out and killed the gunman in the following gun battle. This had just taken place in the past half hour and it happened in the same spot where I normally parked my truck.

I don't know how many times I had parked next to that armored truck, as we always seem to be at the bank at the same time. God had a hand in keeping me from that appointment on that day at that time and He used ants to do that job.

This, along with other events in my life, has taught me to wait for His timing and not charge ahead on my own. If we want to be where God wants us when He wants us, then we must wait to hear His timing.

Another story along this same line is how important it is to get all the love you can, while you have the chance to. I have 3 grown children and 8 grandchildren. When my son was young, we had this great relationship. He would run and jump into my arms all the time and, of course, I loved it. Unfortunately, when he left our home, things were strained between us for many reasons and I didn't get to see him very much over the next few years. I can't tell you how hard this was. My mind and body would literally ache to hold him and feel those hugs. He's grownup and has his own family now and lives halfway across the country and I still can only long for those hugs. It's the same with my daughter. When she was young and I would leave the house without her, she would kick and scream and beat the floor and, when I came home, I would get the look, but then the hugs would come. That pain was and is still very real as I looked back on all the missed opportunities I wasted when they were young and at home. It hurts even more deeply to know that I acted as though those times would last forever.

My word to you if you have young children is get as much of that love as long as they want to give it because there comes a time when it won't be there and you will long for what is no longer available, and it will hurt.

I know that there is a time for our children to grow up and leave home as I know that there is a time for everything, but, until that time, don't waste a hug, enjoy it to the fullest. It's much like the times that our God comes and His presence is so real you feel as though He is hugging you and you don't want it to ever end. Get all of Him you can.

The older I get, the more I understand that it is the same with the *calling* of the Lord. There will be a time when I will have to retire from that also just as I have from the daily work place, but, for right now, there are still days when I know that I can take on the Goliath's of this world and be victorious. Until that time comes to retire from ministry, my desire is to be vital in the work of the kingdom.

So as I have said before, Lord, send me.

What are you saying, Lord, to me?

_____

_____

_____

_____

Draw Near

D raw near to me, oh lonely heart, for I am the lover of your soul. Talk to me, for I will listen and not become tired of your words. Put your head on my chest, for I will care for you. Let me caress your wounds with the warmth of my love for you and let me take the tears from your heart where you have been so hurt. I created you and I know how to heal you so much better than those who wear white coats in long crowded Hospital hallways. Place your trust in me and you will be free to be healed. You were created in My image and likeness so I know you and I know the pain and disappointments that come to you, my child. As I hear you cry out, it is only an echo of my cry for you and my desire to see you whole. My cross meant freedom from the pain and misery you are suffering. The payment was given; now receive the true blessing of the freedom that is yours in Me.

Jesus…..

Duane Harlow

12-16-2004

Contact Information

Rev. Duane Harlow

DuMar Ministries, Inc.

www.DuMarMinistries.com

Dumar888@msn.com

719-550-4575

Other Books by Rev. Duane Harlow

Breaking Out of Religious Christianity

Destiny Image Publishers

The Secret Plan

CPSIA information can be obtained at www.ICGtesting.com
Printed in the USA
LVOW080727300512

283888LV00001B/8/P